Meet Canadian Authors & Illustrators

Revised Edition

60 Creators of Children's Books

ALLISON GERTRIDGE

COVER ILLUSTRATION BY THOMAS DANNENBERG

Scholastic Canada Ltd.

Toronto New York London Auckland Sydney
Mexico City New Delhi Hong Kong

To Lydia, who made me think about sand.

Scholastic Canada Ltd.
175 Hillmount Road, Markham, Ontario L6C 1Z7, Canada

Scholastic Inc.
555 Broadway, New York, NY 10012, USA

Scholastic Australia Pty Limited
PO Box 579, Gosford, NSW 2250, Australia

Scholastic New Zealand Limited
Private Bag 94407, Greenmount, Auckland, New Zealand

Scholastic Ltd.
Villiers House, Clarendon Avenue, Leamington Spa,
Warwickshire CV32 5PR, UK

National Library of Canada Cataloguing in Publication Data

Gertridge, Allison
Meet Canadian authors and illustrators

Rev. ed.
ISBN 0-439-98780-6

1. Authors, Canadian — 20th century — Biography.
2. Illustrators — Canada — Biography. 3. Children's literature, Canadian — Bio-bibliography.
4. Illustration of books — Canada — Bio-bibliography. I. Title.

PS8081.G37 2002   C810.9'9282   C2001-902737-0
PR9186.2.G37 2002

Designed by Andrea Casault

6 5 4 3 2 1   Printed in Canada   02 03 04 05 06

CONTENTS

INTRODUCTION & ACKNOWLEDGEMENTS 5

MICHAEL BEDARD 6

ERIC BEDDOWS 8

PHILIPPE BÉHA 10

JO ELLEN BOGART 12

PAULETTE BOURGEOIS 14

KARLEEN BRADFORD 16

RON BRODA 18

MARGARET BUFFIE 20

BRENDA CLARK 22

SYLVIE DAIGNEAULT 24

KADY MACDONALD DENTON 26

BRIAN DOYLE 28

CHRISTIANE DUCHESNE 30

SARAH ELLIS 32

EUGENIE FERNANDES 34

KIM FERNANDES 36

SHEREE FITCH 38

MARIE-LOUISE GAY 40

PHOEBE GILMAN 42

LINDA GRANFIELD 44

BARBARA GREENWOOD 46

MONICA HUGHES 48

BERNICE THURMAN HUNTER 50

JULIE JOHNSTON 52

RUKHSANA KHAN 54

GORDON KORMAN 56

MARYANN KOVALSKI 58

PAUL KROPP 60

MICHAEL ARVAARLUK KUSUGAK 62

KIM LAFAVE 64

JULIE LAWSON 66

DENNIS LEE 68

MICHÈLE LEMIEUX 70

Continued

Ron Lightburn 72

Jean Little 74

Janet Lunn 76

Claire Mackay 78

Kevin Major 80

Michael Martchenko 82

Carol Matas 84

Norah McClintock 86

Tololwa M. Mollel 88

Robin Muller 90

Robert Munsch 92

Kenneth Oppel 94

Kit Pearson 96

Stéphane Poulin 98

Karen Reczuch 100

Barbara Reid 102

Barbara Smucker 104

Ted Staunton 106

Shelley Tanaka 108

Cora Taylor 110

Maxine Trottier 112

Ian Wallace 114

Eric Walters 116

Eric Wilson 118

Janet Wilson 120

Tim Wynne-Jones 122

Werner Zimmermann 124

Awards 126

Hosting an Author/Illustrator Visit 128

Authors' and Illustrators' Birthdays 131

On Becoming a Better Writer 132

On Becoming a Better Artist 134

Books for Your Classroom Publishing Centre 135

Additional Resources on Specific Authors and Illustrators 136

Photography Credits 140

INTRODUCTION

Here we go again! There are many new faces in this revised edition, and I have again just managed to scratch the surface of who's who in kids' books today. I hope, however, that you will find this to be a rich sampling of what's great about Canadian books for kids.

It's been seven years since the first edition of *Meet Canadian Authors and Illustrators* was published, and since then a great deal is new in the world of children's book publishing. Computer technology has changed everything, from typesetting to design, from printing to distribution. Interestingly enough, though, technology has done little to change the fundamental ways that authors write and that illustrators illustrate.

Most of the authors and illustrators I've interviewed, in fact, consider their computers as a kind of high-tech pencil — it's excellent for editing and reworking, but really hasn't changed the writing process much. Ideas are still collected, considered and developed in much the same way as they always have been. Artists, too, still tend to use the old-standby sketchbooks and library picture files — along with Internet research — when collecting reference material.

Another thing that hasn't changed since the first edition is the advice that the authors and illustrators in this book have for young writers and artists: If you want to be an author, read and write. If you want to be an illustrator, observe and draw.

I hope this collection will not only inspire people to explore the quality books created by this country's greatest talents, but also provide them with practical activities for sharpening their own skills as writers and illustrators. Enjoy!

Acknowledgements

There were many people who helped pull together covers and permissions for this undertaking. My thanks go to: Tom Briggs, Marie Campbell, Kellie Cullihall, Carolyn Deardon, Sophie Deschenes, Lorraine Drolet, Abby Gainforth, Kristen Gough, Fiona Harvey, Valerie Hatton, Samantha Haywood, Agnes Huguet, Akka Janssen, Kate Lennard, Libby Lightstone, Karen McMullin, Marg Anne Morrison, Lisa Nave, Marie Peters, Debra Shapiro, Jessica Strom, Eva Svec, Sue Tate, Jamie Terranova, Matt Williams, Krista Willis and Gail Winskill.

Special thanks go to the book's art director, Andrea Casault, who made everything look so good, and to my editor, Joanne Richter, for her endless patience.

MICHAEL BEDARD

Born: June 26, 1949,
in Toronto, Ontario

Home: Toronto, Ontario

SELECTED TITLES

A Darker Magic — 1987

The Lightning Bolt — 1989

Redwork — 1990
(CLA Book of the Year for Children,
Governor General's Award)

The Tinder Box — 1990

The Nightingale — 1991

Emily — 1992

The Divide — 1997

Glass Town — 1997

The Clay Ladies — 1999

The Wolf of Gubbio — 2000

Michael Bedard didn't do a lot of reading when he was a boy; he confesses that the most involved he became with his copy of *Tom Sawyer* was the time he spent one sunny afternoon burning a hole in its cover with a magnifying glass.

It wasn't until Michael was seventeen that he was bitten by the writing bug. His introduction to the craft was through poetry. "I had a teacher that year who was mad keen about poetry. Being in the presence of someone who was himself really in love with the shapes and sounds of words caught me just at the right point. During the course of that year I discovered a number of people, like T.S. Eliot, [Emily] Dickinson and William Blake. I began writing, and it didn't take too long before I began to fall in love with what I call the taste of words on the tongue, and by the end of that year I was writing poetry."

In fact, Michael became so serious about poetry that he skipped his grade-twelve math exam in order to spend time at the local library reading Dylan Thomas!

Poetry was not what Michael decided to write, though; he would write novels. He received a number of rejections for his first effort, and so decided to put that premier novel aside and begin working on his second, *A Darker Magic*. "Often the first book — a big book like that — is sort of a seed book. You dig down and

you get all of these things out. I've gone back and I've used bits and pieces of that book in things that I've done afterwards, but the book itself will probably never see the light."

Michael uses a lot of reference material to direct his writing; his collections have become so extensive that he needs two offices to accommodate them all. "When I begin to work on a piece, I build a wall above my desk — and it's a wall of pictures that relate to the piece I'm working on. For instance, when I started work on *Redwork*, I put up various pictures of people in magazines who might have reminded me something of the characters I was working on, pictures of various alchemical things I might have come across. I find that with each book that I work on, I tend to put pictures up on the wall to sort of lead me into the book."

THE HAND-HEART CONNECTION

Michael prefers to work in a room with a door that he can close, and he always writes with a pencil in notebooks. He describes what he calls the "hand-heart connection," which he experiences when writing a first draft in longhand. "I think your personality comes across in the actual writing if you write with a pencil, much more than if you were to go directly to type. When words come out in type you tend to be seduced by the look of the type; things look much more finished than they are. The tendency is to be satisfied with less than your best work."

> "I think a large part of what makes one a writer is not just dealing with the good times when words are coming, but being able to persist through the times when nothing is coming."

What does Michael strive to achieve in his best work? "When I work on a piece, I'm careful not to say everything. Less is better when I'm writing. If I can leave things out, then I do, because I think it's very important to leave spaces for the reader to participate by fleshing it out with his or her

Emily
by Michael Bedard · pictures by Barbara Cooney

own imagination. The book is not complete until the reader comes to it; it's not something that you stand back and look at, like a piece of art; it's something that you enter into and complete.

"It's important that readers realize that a book is not like watching television where it's all done for you. What you bring to it is vitally important.

"I think it was Joseph Campbell who said that you should follow your bliss, and I believe that's true. For me, writing is my bliss, and the favourite part of it is following that bliss and seeing where it will lead me. There's a profound joy for me in creating something beyond myself."

DO IT YOURSELF!

Michael Bedard often reflects on the images he brings to the books he reads. Try it yourself. Read something, then close the book and think about what you've read. Picture it in your mind. Then go back to the book and look for differences between the words you have read and the images in your head. What have you added to the passage from your own imagination that wasn't described on the page?

ERIC BEDDOWS

Born: November 29, 1951,
in Woodstock, Ontario

Home: Stratford, Ontario

SELECTED TITLES

Zoom at Sea — 1983
(Amelia Frances Howard-Gibbon Award,
Ruth Schwartz Award)

Zoom Away — 1985
(Amelia Frances Howard-Gibbon Award)

Joyful Noise — 1987

Night Cars — 1988
(Elizabeth Mrazik-Cleaver Award)

Shadow Play — 1990

*Who Shrank My
Grandmother's House?* — 1992

Zoom Upstream — 1992

The Rooster's Gift — 1996
(Governor General's Award)

Circus — 1997

*The Dictionary of
Imaginary Places* — 1999

When he was in school, Eric Beddows was an ambitious reader. "The biggest book in the school library was Darwin's *Voyage of the Beagle* — 'big' in the sense of being the thickest book — so I decided to read that, because I thought everyone would be quite impressed. I don't think anyone was quite impressed, but it got me really interested in science and evolution which is still one of my main interests."

Eric (a.k.a. Ken Nutt) was more particular about choosing his illustrators, however. "In my school books, I actually kept lists of illustrators I liked and didn't like — like baseball cards or sports heroes — only mine were Walter Crane and Rockwell Kent. But I didn't really think about becoming an illustrator myself until Tim Wynne-Jones asked me to illustrate *Zoom at Sea*."

> *"Never think that any piece of time is too small to get your artwork done."*

Those illustrations, like his other work, have a very special appeal for Eric's young fans. Kids often ask him how he makes his pictures look so real. He tells them, "As a child, I didn't like it when an illustrator glossed over things or didn't bother to fill something in. My desire was

always to make a picture feel like you could walk into it, and the way to do that is to know everything about the day that you're drawing. Is it sunny? Is it chilly? Is the wind blowing? Know all the little things, even though they seem like they're not important to the story, because we're always in weather and we're always in light or darkness."

To achieve this desired realism, Eric has run and participated in life-drawing classes every week for more than twenty years. He also does a lot of picture research and keeps clippings in an idea file for quick reference. So, although Zoom in the Zoom books was based on author Tim Wynne-Jones's cat, Montezuma, the cat you see in the books was actually modelled after a picture of a cat from Eric's idea file.

TOO MANY IDEAS

Eric rarely runs out of ideas. In fact, he's more often faced with the problem of having too many. He recalls reading a favourite artist's description of a nightmare in which before his eyes he saw all of the pictures he wasn't going to have time to paint, and insists that he has the same dream all the time.

To decide which ideas to discard, Eric does some careful thinking. "To get back on track, I have to get back to the basics of what I'm trying to say with this book. You can't do all things."

Eric's favourite part of illustrating a book comes after he's made those first decisions and is already into a job. "The illustrations pass a point where they take on a life of their own. It always reminds me of pushing a big rock up a hill. It's really hard to do until it gets to the top, and then it starts to roll down and it's really easy and really fun and a lot happens."

Eric's advice for young artists is: "Keep drawing if you like drawing. A person doesn't sit down and make one drawing from beginning to end. It's a process. It's something that you do over and over. So, if you enjoy doing it and if you keep doing it, you're most of the way there."

Incidentally, Eric has one other bit of information to share with his readers. There is a secret story in *Zoom Upstream*; it's written in code on the endpapers. He suggests that interested sleuths solve the upper left-hand side of the puzzle for a clue to the code. Happy hunting!

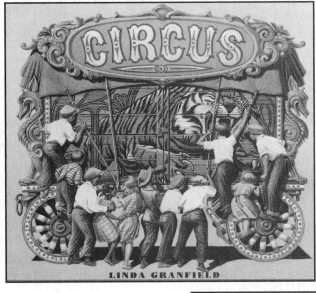

DO IT YOURSELF!!

When Eric Beddows is happy with his drawings, he uses tracing paper to keep the best parts, then transfers them onto good paper. He suggests you draw something once — a dragon, for instance — then rip off its head, legs and tail. (You can do this with a photocopy instead of your original drawing if you'd like.) Then move the pieces around on a blank sheet of paper and you'll find it gives you all kinds of surprising ideas, positions and postures. When you find one you like, tape the pieces down and trace the whole thing onto tracing paper. Then repeat the process with that drawing, and so on. The main thing is not to get too attached to your own drawing, and to try new things.

PHILIPPE BÉHA

Born: January 1, 1950,
in Casablanca, Morocco

Home: Montreal, Quebec

SELECTED TITLES

*Le voyage à la
recherche du temps* — 1980

Seul au monde — 1982

*Par la bave de mon
crapaud* — 1985

Moulitou — 1987

Voyage au bout du monde — 1988

Les Jeux de Pic-Mots
(Governor General's Award)

*What Do the Fairies Do with
All Those Teeth?* — 1989
(Mr. Christie's Book Award)

Toto la brute — 1992

Biscuits in the Cupboard — 1998
(Mr. Christie's Book Award)

Creative Crafts for Critters — 2001

Philippe Béha can't seem to find enough time to illustrate. After a busy eight-hour day in his studio, he takes a break to spend the evening with his wife and daughters; then, while his family sleeps, he's back at his table, often working right through the night. Needless to say, Philippe does not need a lot of sleep!

It's no wonder, though, that he keeps such long hours. Philippe likes to have as many as ten projects on the go, and during his career as a professional illustrator he has illustrated more than one hundred books!

> *"In illustration you can make anything happen. Unlike photography, you don't need a set-up, a camera or an assistant. All you need is a good idea, something to draw with, and you can create anything you want."*

Describing himself as "an excited child," Philippe quickly becomes absorbed in each new project. He works fast, taking only a couple of hours to complete even his most complex illustrations. He even completed the pictures for his award-winning book *What Do the Fairies Do with All Those Teeth?* in what is surely a record-breaking two days. That includes the rough sketches and all of the paintings! Fantastic feats like this make some of his friends wonder if he's from another planet.

Philippe doesn't concentrate his efforts on illustrating only for kids, though. His vibrant illustrations have found their place in posters, advertisements and magazines for readers of all ages.

SECRET RECIPES

Philippe is known for his ability to draw in many different styles. He works in watercolours, but it's what he mixes with his paints that makes his technique so unusual. "At first, I just worked with water, but later I began experimenting with whatever I found around the house. I'll often spend the entire night in the kitchen trying different mixtures. Sometimes nothing comes of it, but once in a while I hit something great. If it suits the illustration, I'll use it once, maybe twice, and then never use it again."

Philippe won't reveal any of his special secret recipes, but teases that it could be anything from eggs to orange juice! He rarely uses the same combination more than twice because each of his books is so different that it simply wouldn't look right.

"Sometimes I can use the same thing, but generally I want to try new things. If it surprises me, I know it will surprise my readers."

His favourite part of doing an illustration is thinking up the ideas, Philippe says, and he explains that the faster they come, the better they are. "It's like a game. I start and I say, in ten minutes I must have a good concept." He almost always comes up with one. After years of practice and so many projects, Philippe says some of the things he comes up with still surprise him!

Philippe will take on just about any project that comes his way, all the while looking for new challenges and new ways to experiment with style and technique. "You get to a point where nothing scares you — and that makes it fun. There isn't a challenge I won't take on. Time, experience and success give you a

Biscuits in the Cupboard

Barbara Nichol

Illustrated by Philippe Beha

certain self-assurance. Once you're committed, you'll always find a way."

MICHEL LUPPENS

PHILIPPE BÉHA

What do the fairies do with all those teeth?

Do It Yourself!

Take some inspiration from Philippe Béha's midnight concoctions and experiment by mixing different things into your watercolour paints. You could, for instance, try sand, cornstarch, salt or crayon shavings to see how these things alter the colour and texture. Anything goes!

JO ELLEN BOGART

Born: October 20, 1945,
in Houston, Texas, USA

Home: Guelph, Ontario

SELECTED TITLES

Dylan's Lullaby — 1988

Malcolm's Runaway Soap — 1988

Ten for Dinner — 1989

Daniel's Dog — 1990

Sarah Saw a Blue Macaw — 1991

Mama's Bed — 1993

Gifts — 1994

Jeremiah Learns to Read — 1997
(Ruth Schwartz Award)

*Money: Make It,
Spend It, Save It* — 2001

*The Night the
Stars Flew* — 2001

When she was a child, Jo Ellen Bogart recalls, her mother encouraged her to make beautiful picture books. Still, Jo Ellen didn't decide to become an author until she moved to Canada in 1975. More than ten years later, the manuscripts for her books *Dylan's Lullaby* and *Malcolm's Runaway Soap* were accepted for publication by two different editors.

True to her mother's words, Jo Ellen continues to make beautiful books, drawing on her family, friends and especially pets for ideas. "My experience has been that picture book ideas come on their own if I wait patiently and open my mind. Most poems and stories I write take just a few hours. Then, weeks later, I might pick them up and work on some polishing."

And what about those odd occasions when Jo Ellen decides to play hooky? "I do housework. To put off doing housework, I read or play with my pets. When I'm very restless, I drive out into the country and watch cows and horses and sheep. I love to hear the sounds they make in the quiet, and I love to be able to see for long distances. I guess it reminds me of Texas where I grew up."

A REAL ANIMAL LOVER

In fact, Jo Ellen has always enjoyed being around animals, at one time or another sharing her home with a coatimundi named Clyde (look for him in *Sarah Saw a Blue Macaw*), TorTor, an Argentine desert tortoise which ran loose around the house, an African clawed frog named Astro, a chipmunk named Alvin which was rescued from a trap, forty mice, assorted gerbils, guinea pigs, water turtles and the occasional salamander. She even spent time in South America with her zoologist husband, studying creatures of the rainforest and taking pictures which would eventually inspire her book, *Sarah Saw a Blue Macaw*.

> *"Making a story happen is like filling an empty space. There was nothing there before you started, and when you finish, there is something."*

Further inspiration for that book came when Jo Ellen was teaching speech therapy in a remedial school. There, she and her students would play around with sentences that used irregular verbs in different tenses. "With my mind in that set I heard myself say, 'Sarah saw a blue macaw.' This happens a lot. I hear the title in my head and from that the story will go."

After writing the first draft of a poem that was full of irregular verbs and began with the question, "What did Sarah

see?" Jo Ellen talked to her editor at Scholastic. Together they decided to change the story from one whose characters lived in a city neighbourhood to one about rainforest animals in their natural environment. Jo Ellen stuck with the irregular verbs and with her question and answer format, but the fact that she could no longer talk about bicycles and other civilized things made finding rhyming words a lot trickier. "Every restriction made the target smaller. It was like an enormous puzzle."

But puzzle it out she did, managing to achieve a personal goal along the way — creating a book that would be translated into Spanish, a language she herself has studied. "Sometimes it's good to be flexible. We worked together and came up with a good book."

Jo Ellen has two pieces of advice for interested young authors. The first is to read as much as you can. "Reading provides such a wonderful supply of ideas and language and of other people's thoughts and experiences."

The second piece of advice is to "mull over" what you have seen or read or done or felt. "Mulling is rolling around words and images in your head. From the outside, it looks a lot like daydreaming. The next step might be to mull on paper. Getting your own thoughts down where you can look at them again is good. Sooner or later something good, something you really like, will appear in these writings."

When asked to describe her favourite part of writing stories and poems, Jo Ellen replies, "My favourite part is the sheer enjoyment of making something up and liking it. The next good part is having people say that they like what I have written. Being able to make a career of writing and have a lot of freedom with my time is wonderful." Though she admits, "Not having regular daily contact with people in a working environment can be lonely."

DO IT YOURSELF!

Here's a tall-tale writing idea from Jo Ellen Bogart. Write a letter to an imaginary friend to tell that friend what's happening in your life — or in your cousin's life, or your dog's life, or your iguana's life (even if you don't have an iguana). If the truth needs rearranging, do it. If made-up parts make the story better, add them. Throw your ingredients into the pot and stir!

PAULETTE BOURGEOIS

Born: July 20, 1951,
in Winnipeg, Manitoba

Home: Toronto, Ontario

SELECTED TITLES

Franklin in the Dark — 1986

The Amazing Apple Book — 1987

Big Sarah's Little Boots — 1987

Hurry Up, Franklin — 1989

*In My Neighbourhood:
Canadian Fire Fighters* — 1991

Franklin Is Bossy — 1993

*Starting with Space:
The Moon* — 1995

Finders Keepers for Franklin — 1997

Franklin's Baby Sister — 2000

Oma's Quilt — 2001

Paulette Bourgeois recalls, "I was once told by my grade-ten English teacher that I could write well, and I've never forgotten it. I wonder what would have happened if somebody had said I could play basketball well!"

Although she says this in jest — Paulette insists she's too short to play basketball! — she does suspect that when she was in school, she spent too much time with her nose in a book and not enough time trying other things, particularly athletic things.

But maybe all of that reading was the thing that got her hooked on writing in the first place. Paulette has made quite a name for herself by writing picture book stories about a shy turtle named Franklin, but she's also created all sorts of kid-friendly information books on everything from dirt to apples. "I love finding out things. I have research and interviewing skills, and I like to use them."

Paulette describes her first publishing experience this way: "It was exciting to have a book to send, disappointing when I received my first six rejections, thrilling to have it accepted and frustrating to have to keep on working at it."

WRITING BEGETS WRITING

She does keep working at it, though. "Writing begets writing!" says Paulette. So, even when she's really struggling with a piece,

Paulette stays in her office, where she reads or works on one of the other two or three projects she has going. "Sometimes, though, if I find I'm blocked on something for days and days and days on end, I seriously question whether I know where I'm going in the story and whether the story is worth writing."

Often Paulette has help in making these initial decisions. "Each of my non-fiction topics is suggested by my publisher. Then I decide on the outline, on how I'm going to research it and what's going to be included. I try to think about what I would have wanted to know about the subject when I was a kid."

When she's working on a new non-fiction book, Paulette requires about four months just to do the research, which isn't surprising given the kinds of questions she needs to answer.

"In *The Amazing Dirt Book*, I had to answer the question: Do people ever eat dirt and why? That was a tricky one. But I'm very lucky to have a research library close by which is connected by computer to a large database. I asked the librarian to do the search for me, then I got a lot of journals and articles to read about that topic." (For those of you who are curious, people from more than two hundred cultures eat dirt. You'll have to read Paulette's book to learn more about dirt eating, a practice she doesn't recommend!)

When it's time to begin writing, Paulette believes in being organized. "I spend at least a week making a detailed outline, and then I work to the outline. I rarely stray and I do at least one major and two or three minor revisions. Then we get experts to read the book, and there's usually one more major edit required."

> "Having somebody that you admire and respect tell you that you've done something well makes an enormous impact."

Paulette says that the ideas for her Franklin books come from her own childhood memories, but they also come from overhearing conversations or from books, magazines and newspapers. Franklin was not inspired by a pet turtle, as Paulette has never had a turtle of her own.

Oma's Quilt

Paulette Bourgeois
Stéphane Jorisch

"Most of my work is getting ideas, and that I do sitting in front of a fire or in the summer at my cottage where I look out at the ocean and the sand dunes. Also, it's amazing the number of ideas I get going to the symphony. I guess listening to the music jogs ideas. It's just a peaceful time to think." In fact, Paulette is so serious about the inspiration music gives her that she doesn't listen to music while she works, for fear that too many ideas will come through and make it hard for her to focus.

People often say to Paulette, "Writing must be so hard because you're alone all the time." But that couldn't be farther from the truth. "I think people generally forget that you *choose* to spend time alone. I like it — I think I need it."

DO IT YOURSELF!

If you have trouble ending your stories, why not start your story at the end? Paulette Bourgeois suggests you make up a great last line and then work backwards, asking yourself questions like, How could this happen? Whom did this happen to? What were those characters like?

KARLEEN BRADFORD

Born: December 13, 1936,
in Toronto, Ontario

Home: Owen Sound, Ontario

SELECTED TITLES

Wrong Again, Robbie — 1977

I Wish There Were Unicorns — 1983

*The Haunting
at Cliff House* — 1985

The Nine Days Queen — 1986

Windward Island — 1989

There Will Be Wolves — 1992
(CLA Young Adult Book Award)

Write Now! — 1996

*A Different Kind
of Champion* — 1998

Whisperings of Magic — 2001

Animal Heroes — 2001

"I don't know that I ever knew I was meant to be a writer, but I've always loved writing. Absolutely as far back as I can remember, my favourite activity was curling up in a corner somewhere with a book at school. I loved anything to do with books and writing."

It wasn't long before Karleen Bradford was putting her favourite pastime into practice. She thinks back, "Around grade four I can remember writing plays. I can remember walking down the school corridor, and I had my latest play in my hand. I saw a group of my friends coming towards me, and I heard this loud whisper, 'Oh, no! Karleen's written another play and she's going to make us act in it. Run! Hide!' I do remember that I got them and I did make them act in it!"

WELL-TRAVELLED AND WELL-RESEARCHED

Karleen Bradford was born in Toronto, but moved with her parents to Argentina when she was nine years old. She returned to Canada to attend the University of Toronto and to marry a foreign service officer with the Canadian government. Together he and Karleen would spend thirty-four years travelling, living in Colombia, the United States, England, the Philippines, Brazil, Germany and Puerto Rico.

It seems inevitable, then, that a trip would start Karleen writing her first historical book. While visiting Upper Canada Village with her kids, she found herself alone in the old schoolhouse. Karleen remembers looking at "the scarred desks, the ancient blackboard, the wooden steps worn smooth by the shoes of children from over one hundred years before" and suddenly wondering, "What if a young Canadian girl of today, on a school field trip, wandered in here and was suddenly transported back in time to when the school was new and full of students?"

And so the premise for *The Other Elizabeth* was born. In the book, a girl named Elizabeth Duncan visits Upper Canada Village with her grade-seven class. There, she becomes Elizabeth Frobisher and is caught up in the

events of a time very different from her own.

It would be the first of many heavily researched and highly entertaining books Karleen would write for young people, most of them inspired by places she has visited on her travels. She has travelled specifically for her writing, too. For instance, for her books about the crusades, Karleen and her husband retraced the crusaders' footsteps from Cologne, Germany, to Istanbul, Turkey.

> *"At school I thought history was just a bunch of dates and dead people."*

In addition to developing her own stories, Karleen has written a book on the writing process entitled *Write Now!* She also teaches creative writing — in person and over the Internet — and she maintains an excellent Web site with all kinds of information for writers.

She explains, "I realized that having a Web site was a valuable tool for a writer. Besides, I was intrigued with the idea.

"I get a lot of e-mail from teachers and students from the Web site. Teachers are often interested in the how-to of writing and how best to work with their students. Students who are doing projects or novel studies will often write to me with questions about my life, writing habits, sources for stories, methods of research and other details. I refer them first to the FAQs (frequently asked questions) page, but encourage them to write again with any questions that may not have been dealt with on that page."

Karleen's presence on the Internet doesn't stop there: she's recently signed a deal with an electronic publisher who will be selling digital "copies" of some of her books on-line.

And although she's excited about this foray into the world of electronic publishing, Karleen doesn't think it will ever replace the printed word.

"I can't believe that will ever happen. I think there is a place for both kinds of publishing."

DO IT YOURSELF!

Karleen Bradford's travels have inspired many of her books. The next time you go on a trip, take notes and pictures and collect maps and brochures to help you remember as much as you can about your visit. Then when you return home, refer to your file of nformation and use that place as the setting for your next story.

RON BRODA

Born: May 26, 1954,
in New Hamburg, Ontario

Home: Sarnia, Ontario

SELECTED TITLES

*The Little Crooked
Christmas Tree* — 1990

Caterpillar Magic — 1991

Blue Jay Babies — 1991

Waters — 1993

Spider's Lunch — 1995

Have You Seen Bugs? — 1996

3-D Paper Crafts — 1997

*Dinosaur: Digging Up
a Giant* — 1999

Butterflies — 2000

The sixth child in a family of eleven children, Ron Broda was not a great reader when he was in school. In fact, he had so much trouble reading as a kid that he avoided it whenever he could. He preferred instead to pursue the unusual hobby of collecting animals. "I used to be one of those children who, after school, went through bushes chasing anything that would run, or crawl in a hole, or fly. I tried to get as close as I could, thinking I could catch it."

And indeed he did. "I had everything. The most pigeons I had at one time was about 240. And then I had ducks and chickens and rabbits and groundhogs. I kept them all as pets."

It may not be a coincidence, then, that Ron does such a great job of sculpting animals in paper. Even in those early years he was experimenting with the medium — he fondly recalls cutting out paper cats to decorate the windows for Halloween. "I was a real animal person."

HIS OWN PERSONAL STYLE

After putting himself through art college as the drummer in a band, Ron received a gift from a friend: a poster featuring an illustration made entirely out of paper sculpture. He was so taken with the look of the piece that he decided to experiment with the medium in earnest, and eventually developed his own personal style.

"When I went through college, I thought you were born with a style. None of the teachers ever said you should develop a style and try different things. Sooner or later, though, you try everything and you play with everything and there's suddenly one medium that you enjoy."

When kids ask Ron, How did you do that?, he finds it hard to provide them with a detailed answer. His quick explanation of how he works with paper is: "I cut and fold it with my hands, and curl it with different instruments like scissors."

But much more than that is involved in creating the stunning three-dimensional pieces that make up Ron's books. He's always fine-tuning his craft and even uses materials other than paper, on occasion, to achieve a desired effect. For instance, in his

book *Waters*, Ron used a glue gun and cut up pieces of acetate to make melting snow, spider's webs and icicles. When the pieces were photographed for the book, the lights glistened through the built-up acetate and made his pictures seem more realistic.

Instead of buying paper in hundreds of different colours, Ron usually begins with plain white watercolour paper. Then he tints the paper with watercolour paints, creating exactly the colours he wants. This also makes it possible for him to paint details like eyes on his creatures when he's finished sculpting.

> *"Don't think, I haven't got [a personal style] yet and it's getting to that time when I'll need it. It will come."*

A small picture can take as many as twelve hours to do. So when Ron is working on a particularly difficult piece, he's careful not to let himself get overwhelmed. "I treat it as a puzzle, doing one piece at a time. If I'm not really into it one day, I'll get at least one piece done, and the next day I'll get another piece done, and before you know it I'm getting a lot of pieces done and two weeks are gone and it's almost finished."

Ron draws sketches for the entire book first. Then he begins the paper sculpture, starting with the pages that excite him the least, and saving his favourites for last. This keeps him enthusiastic about the job right up until it's finished. "You've got to keep that positive feeling going all the time!"

DO IT YOURSELF!

Ron Broda suggests you keep a sketchbook and draw for at least five minutes, but not more than ten minutes, every day. It won't be hard to get in the habit because it's such a short time to work, but over time it will make a big difference in helping you to develop your own personal style.

MARGARET BUFFIE

Born: March 29, 1945,
in Winnipeg, Manitoba

Home: Winnipeg, Manitoba

SELECTED TITLES

Who Is Frances Rain? — 1987
(CLA Young Adult Book Award)

The Guardian Circle — 1989

My Mother's Ghost — 1989

The Dark Garden — 1995

Angels Turn Their Backs — 1998

The Watcher — 2000

Vicky Metcalf Award winner, 1996

"I think I always knew that someday I would write a book," Margaret Buffie recalls. "The seed of this ambition was sown by my grade-four teacher, Miss Day. I can remember when she handed me back one of my stories; she told me she was sure I would be a writer some day and that stuck in my brain. I never forgot her enthusiastic encouragement. After she said that, I always believed that I could do it."

That belief in herself has taken Margaret a long way. Her first book was accepted by a publisher just two weeks after it was submitted, which is possibly a world record! "The whole experience was both frightening and terribly exciting. In fact, I jumped up and down after I hung up the phone, and I put my back out for two days. It was an exquisite pain!"

But while Margaret was confident about writing from the beginning, she was not prepared for editing. "The thing I had to do before I would be able to have the book published was to work with an editor and shorten the book by about fifty pages, and that was a really terrifying prospect. But I was encouraged and applauded by both my editor and my publisher throughout the whole process. It's funny, when I finally saw the finished books I was in absolute awe and I remember asking myself, Who did this? I really didn't think I

could have done it myself!"

Margaret has developed a number of techniques for revising her work, but one of the most important is used to develop dialogue. "Sometimes the changes come easily, but sometimes I have to 'talk' with my characters and let them have a say in where exactly I've gone wrong. This happens during the revision process. If your characters aren't saying the right things, then you have to get to know them a little bit better and let them say what they want to say. If something is stilted or unnatural, then you know your words are shaping it and not the characters'."

"I always find it intriguing to ask people where they get their ideas from."

Readers often ask Margaret if she plans to write other books using the same characters. Margaret replies, *"The Guardian Circle* has an ending that offers a possible sequel, but I've found that sequels to movies and to other books are often a disappointment, so I think that I'll only do a sequel to *The Guardian Circle* if I get a new idea that will be as strong and full of action as the first book, and if I feel strongly compelled to spend a year writing it."

In the meantime, however, there are many more things to write about; Margaret never seems to run out of ideas. "If anything, I wish I was three people so I could set us all in front of a computer and say: Okay, here it is. Get going!"

ON A ROLL

"I definitely have a tendency to procrastinate, but once I do bypass all of these things and sit down and get to work, it's very hard to take a break. I usually become so involved in it. There are many days when the story that I'm working on is really going so well that I sit down at nine and I have to be dragged away from it. I even eat my lunch over the keyboard!"

Perhaps part of the reason Margaret becomes so involved in her work is that she identifies so much with the subject matter. The setting for Margaret's first book, *Who Is Frances Rain?*, was based on her own cottage experiences. "I had gone to a cottage like Gran's all of my life, and because I'd painted and photographed it so much over the years, I really felt that I knew what it smelt like and what it looked like. Because it was such an important part of my life experience, I really wanted to write a book about it."

The rest of Margaret's inspiration for that novel came when she was digging around on an island near that same cottage. As she worked to clear the land of an old garbage dump, she came across a jug containing an old pair of spectacles and the question came to her: What would happen if I put them on and was able to look into the past?

From that one question an entire story evolved. So the next time you run out of ideas, you may want to try doing the very same thing: ask yourself a question to get the ball rolling.

DO IT YOURSELF!

Plan and prepare a combination diary/ sketchbook just as Frances Rain's daughter did in Margaret Buffie's book *Who Is Frances Rain?* You could either create one for Frances Rain's daughter based on the information you collect from the book, or you could create one for yourself, collecting information and pictures over a number of months or years.

BRENDA CLARK

Born: February 10, 1955,
in Toronto, Ontario

Home: Nestleton, Ontario

SELECTED TITLES

Sadie and the Snowman — 1985

Franklin in the Dark — 1986

Big Sarah's Little Boots — 1987

Puddleman — 1988

Little Fingerling — 1989

Hurry Up, Franklin — 1989

My Dog — 1993

Franklin Is Lost — 1992

Franklin's New Friend — 1997

Franklin and Harriet — 2001

Looking back on her childhood, Brenda Clark comments, "I didn't read enough and I have to make up for it now. Reading is good because you get all these images in your mind, and it just helps you draw better. Take my word for it — it works!"

What little reading Brenda did do when she was young happened at school. "I really liked the school readers. I remember looking at those pictures and wondering about who drew them. I was actually inspired by those first readers, believe it or not."

And what came next for this artist who had spent her early years gazing at the pictures in her school readers? "My first published pieces were for readers. Which was, for me, a dream come true. It was something I'd always wondered about. It was really exciting to see something printed, and I still get that same feeling after all these years."

Brenda admits that, despite the thrill of seeing her work in print, she is sometimes disappointed by the way the colours in her paintings change when they're printed in books. Over the years she has, however, found ways to get around this common illustrator's complaint. "When I first started out, I experimented with pencil crayons and chalks and different coloured papers, but I found that, for me, watercolours reproduced the brightest. I don't use watercolours

like a watercolourist. I use water really sparingly, so it's mostly just the colour you see. I build up from the lightest colours to the darkest colours. This is called glazing."

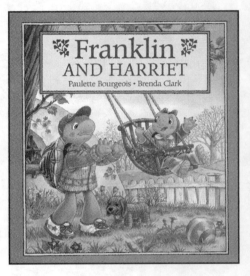

Brenda believes in being prepared when she begins a new project. "I love doing research, I really do. And I think it probably helps a lot when I get projects like *Little Fingerling*, for instance. I needed to portray accurately the Japanese lifestyle of long ago and I couldn't make that up. So I did months of research at the Royal Ontario Museum. They have a Far East library there, so I had access to actual Japanese art and artifacts throughout the whole nine months that it took me to do the book."

TIPS FROM A FAN

In addition to careful research, Brenda values feedback from a number of sources. Once, she received a letter from a boy who wanted to know why the ice in the plastic bag in *Sadie and the Snowman* didn't look like ice. In the book, Sadie wants to keep her snowman over the summer, so she puts her melted friend in the freezer, and the following winter takes out the bag of ice to make a new snowman. "I guess I didn't have the technical ability at that time. He was perfectly right. I made it look like snow instead of ice. It should have been more transparent."

"I don't believe there's any such thing as making a mistake, but I do believe in changes."

Franklin's character, too, took a lot of reworking. Says Brenda, "At first he didn't look like a turtle. When I first brought him in [to the publisher], I was told he looked sort of like a parrot or a lizard. So I literally had to go back to the drawing board and give him more appeal. I added a few human expressions and characteristics so he would stand out from your regular everyday turtle."

Brenda made it work. Today, with a popular cartoon series of his own and his image on everything from toys to backpacks, Franklin certainly does stand out from your everyday turtle.

Brenda often looks to her publisher and the book's author for thoughts on her drawings. "They go over them and I just wait to see what their comments are. I hope they have suggestions because I'm always looking for something fresh and because it's hard for one person to see everything. Some of the changes that they suggest may not seem appropriate to me at first, but if I think about them or if I give them a try, often I'm surprised by the improvement."

Brenda's words of advice for people interested in becoming professional illustrators are: "Pretend your mind is a camera and click pictures every chance you get. Try and remember things like patterns, shapes and colours, and keep a sketchbook handy at all times. Then go through your sketchbook every once in a while and pick out your very best sketches. Keep them aside in a portfolio and look back at it and see how much you've improved. It will give you the incentive to keep at it because you will see improvement."

Brenda Clark's books are read to children all around the world. "I never dreamed my illustrations would be seen by so many people. Some of the titles are even seen in faraway places like China and Australia, Belgium and Great Britain, and I often wonder what the children in Hong Kong or Sydney think of Franklin the turtle."

Sadie and the Snowman

By Allen Morgan • Illustrated by Brenda Clark

Do It Yourself!

A little planning can go a long way. Brenda Clark suggests that, before you do the pictures for a book you've written, you work out all the bugs by doing some thumbnail sketches. (Thumbnail sketches are just very small rough drawings of the pictures you plan to do.)

Sketch each picture in a number of different ways: from a bird's-eye view, from a worm's-eye view, from far away or close up. Thumbnail sketches save you from wasting time or paper on angles and ideas that don't work, giving you more time to work on your final illustrations.

SYLVIE DAIGNEAULT

Born: November 28, 1952, in Montreal, Quebec

Home: Toronto, Ontario

SELECTED TITLES

🎨 *Simon's Surprise* — 1986

🎨 *No Dinosaurs in the Park* — 1990

🎨 *Sarah Saw a Blue Macaw* — 1991

🎨 *Mother Nature Takes a Vacation* — 1992

🎨 *Mama's Bed* — 1993

Bruno in the Snow — 1994

Bruno Springs Up — 1997

Bruno and the Bees — 1998

Bruno Falls Asleep — 1999

🎨 *All on a Sleepy Night* — 2001

🎨 — illustrations only

"When I was really young, I remember cutting myself little tiny pieces of paper and making a book. Then I pretended that I was writing. In fact, I was sort of drawing writing because I would go, curl, curl, curl, space, and I did the whole book like that. I was really proud of my book. I used pencil crayons when I made it."

Years later, Sylvie attended a convent school in Montreal. She says, "A nice convent with Italian nuns. At this school everything was oriented to art and performance and music. The art teacher there told me she thought I had a special talent with drawing, and said I could come to the art class and draw whatever I wanted, whenever I had free time. This was in grades two, three and four, so the encouragement started early."

LOOKING AT EVERY ANGLE

After so many years of practice, Sylvie has learned the importance of paying close attention to detail. "I do a lot of research. I go to the library and sometimes I'll take out a hundred pictures for one book. Even though I know how to draw things like flowers, I like to go and look at references because I think your drawings get better when you have more information; otherwise you tend to draw everything the same way. You get comfortable about drawing a dog a certain way or drawing a cat a certain way, and you just stick to it. Sometimes I even have five pictures for the same animal because I want to know how long the tail is and in one picture the tail is not there.

"I like to push my knowledge of drawing."

"I usually spend about a day per linear [original pencil drawing] and the finished art goes between two and four days. I do all of the linears in order because a story has a momentum. It's like reading a book or watching a movie; I don't want to watch the middle of the movie and then go back to the beginning. I usually do the cover last because the cover is supposed to reflect what's inside, and by the time I've done all of the pages, I'm totally familiar with all of the characters and the mood."

Although she began her career using paint as her medium, Sylvie has been using pencil crayons to do her illustrations for more than fifteen years. "I decided one day to go to pencils because it was an easy medium to carry around and it has such a wide variety of colours. I think they also appeal to me because they almost look like sticks of candy."

But using pencil has its own challenges. The colour and texture of the paper, for instance, become really important. Sylvie says, "For *Mama's Bed* I got a whole bunch of cream paper and when all the linears had been done and I'd started colouring, I didn't like the texture. I was not happy at all about the way the pencil was responding with the paper. And I trashed everything and went back and I bought another kind of paper. Paper really changes pencil and I change paper often, depending on what I want to achieve." If you look closely at *Sarah Saw a Blue Macaw*, for example, you can see that every page was drawn on a different paper!

When she finally does achieve a look she likes, Sylvie looks for a second opinion. "My husband is an illustrator, so I'll often show him my sketches and ask what he thinks. You get so close to what you do, you don't quite see if there's something wrong. I like to have another opinion.

"The best way to achieve something unique and strong is by being yourself. It's good to be influenced by other people, but I think it's best to reach a place where you feel really comfortable because it's your work and there's nobody else quite like you."

DO IT YOURSELF!

Sylvie Daigneault suggests you look at a friend, a pet or even a view — then turn away from your subject and try to draw from memory what you've seen.

KADY MACDONALD DENTON

Born: July 22, 1942, in Winnipeg, Manitoba

Home: Brandon, Manitoba

SELECTED TITLES

The Picnic — 1988

Dorothy's Dream — 1989

🎨 *Til All the Stars Have Fallen* — 1989
(Amelia Frances Howard-Gibbon Award)

🎨 *The Story of Little Quack* — 1990
(Mr. Christie's Book Award)

🎨 *Before I Go to Sleep* — 1990

Realms of Gold — 1992

The Kingfisher Children's Bible — 1993

A Child's Treasury of Nursery Rhymes — 1998
(Amelia Frances Howard-Gibbon Award, Elizabeth Mrazik-Cleaver Award, Governor General's Award)

🎨 *The Umbrella Party* — 1998

🎨 *I Wished for a Unicorn* — 2000

🎨 — illustrations only

Kady MacDonald Denton grew up in a family where artistic pursuits were encouraged. She remembers, "My parents and brother and sister and I, we all drew and made things. It wasn't something that was done professionally, but it was a part of our lives. There were always supplies around, and it was considered a valued thing to do to settle down and work on a painting. It didn't really matter what one did. No one said, 'Oh, that's good!' Instead they would say, 'Oh, good for you!' — meaning good for you for putting in the time.

"The first book I wrote and illustrated was *The Picnic*. I remember the editor knew it was my first book all on my own and kindly wrote me an encouraging letter and told me to have fun with it. I thought, Gosh, then I will! It was good advice and I've stuck to it ever since."

Although she has fun with her work, Kady often spends long hours creating pictures in her small home studio. She describes her work style: "I find I go at early work in short attacks — focusing intensely for short periods of time, then letting the ideas set. That stage of the process may take several weeks or months. Final illustrations are different. By that time the plan is firmly in my mind and it's a question of putting in the hours to accomplish it. So I will start early most days. I go into the studio after breakfast and work through the morning. I find it extremely useful to stop and go for quick walks; that sort of shakes up the ideas. On final illustrations I work long hours and focus completely on that world, slipping away from the real world for however long it takes me to finish the book."

Finished, of course, is a relative term. Kady laughs, "You're finished when you run out of time. There really is no other way to put it. Sometimes you know something has been laid down just right and you couldn't improve on it, but there are always pieces for which you think another few days might have been nice.

"I do find it odd sometimes when people think working for

children isn't demanding work. Sometimes if I say I write and illustrate books for children people slow down their speech and enunciate more clearly . . . I find that both amusing and odd. The challenges are different. It is its own field and with different parameters. Any work of art is difficult, but it's not less. It's not a shadow or mini-version of adult work by any means.

> *"I don't define myself by my job. I work as a writer/illustrator, but what interests me is the sort of person I am."*

"My experience has given me great admiration for other illustrators. I know the challenges, and I take great delight in seeing how other people have met those challenges."

Although Kady prefers to "work from life," she still finds herself gathering ideas and hunting for reference material. She explains, "I carry a notepad, but I've put ideas down on the backs of shopping lists or anything that's stuffed in my bag or pocket. And I have files of bits and pieces. I once had to do illustrations of a lot of camels. I could find pictures of camels, but I couldn't find pictures of their feet. They were always in sand. Now — not that I'll ever be asked again, of course — but now I have a hefty file of camels' feet. I prefer to work from life, but camels are hard to come by."

Unlike some children's book authors and illustrators, Kady prefers not to include information about herself in her books. She explains, "My responsibility as an illustrator is to the story I'm given. I don't come into it in that sense. My job is to express the story visually, and it is the story and only the story that's important. The author has told the story in words and I must tell it in pictures, and together we're going to create a unique piece of work."

WORD OF ADVICE

Kady has two important tips for young artists. She says, "First, never worry about what other people are doing, and second, remember you can tear up and throw away anything you don't like. Artists do it all the time. I'm always surprised at how often children don't know that. When I do a class presentation, I will tear up and throw away a drawing right in front of them and they think that's wonderful. I often do it just to show children they're in charge. It's their work."

When students ask Kady where she gets her ideas, she understands the importance of the question. "The short answer, of course, is that ideas come from observation and imagination. But I think what they really mean is, Can I be a writer or an illustrator? Can I find ideas, also? The answer to that is yes. You have your own stories and they do matter and you will have your own way of seeing."

DO IT YOURSELF!

People often mistakenly believe that when you're good at something you just do it, but Kady MacDonald Denton says that isn't true at all. The more you do something, the higher your standards get and the more you throw away. Kady's suggestion: the next time you make a picture you aren't entirely happy with, throw it away and begin again. You are certain to be happier with your next draft or the one after that.

BRIAN DOYLE

Born: August 12, 1935, in Ottawa, Ontario

Home: Ottawa, Ontario

SELECTED TITLES

Hey, Dad! — 1978

You Can Pick Me Up at Peggy's Cove — 1979

Up to Low — 1982
(CLA Book of the Year for Children)

Angel Square — 1987

Easy Avenue — 1988
(CLA Book of the Year for Children)

Covered Bridge — 1990
(Mr. Christie's Book Award)

Spud Sweetgrass — 1992

Spud in Winter — 1995

Uncle Ronald — 1996
(CLA Book of the Year for Children, Mr. Christie's Book Award)

Mary Ann Alice — 2001

Vicky Metcalf Award winner, 1991

Journalism wasn't in the cards for Brian Doyle. Although he graduated from Carlton University in 1957 with a degree in journalism and, soon after, took a job with the *Toronto Telegram*, it would take a mere four months for Brian to reconsider his career choice. Brian Doyle wanted to write for fiction readers. He decided to pursue this goal by becoming a teacher.

It would be a good choice for Brian, allowing him a direct connection with his audience. In his many years as a teacher, Brian wrote, directed and produced many plays and musicals with his students — sometimes coordinating as many as 250 kids in one production.

It's also given Brian the impetus to write many novels for young people, garnering him not only major awards and critical praise, but also a loyal following of dedicated readers. That's not bad for a kid who was once told he wouldn't get anywhere.

Brian remembers acting tough when he was young, to cover the embarrassment of living in poverty. His book *Angel Square* was especially difficult to write, he says, because it is very close to his own childhood. For instance, Brian took his time writing about the sister in the story because she was based on his own sister, Pamela, who had Down's syndrome and died of diphtheria at the age of fourteen.

Brian also recalls struggling at school, failing every course in his grade-nine year except English. But Brian learned that school performance was one area of his life where he could make a positive change. One year, after scoring just 3 percent on a geometry exam, Brian tried again the following term and scored a whopping 99 percent.

He recalls, "It's as though I just suddenly woke up!"

The experience would forever change the way this writer thought about his own schooling, and about the education system as a whole. Brian believes strongly that kids are much brighter than many people think; they simply lack the experience of being able to put their thoughts into words.

This principle shapes his writing, too. "Kids at ten know a lot — they're very wise, although they're not slippery, not good enough liars yet. A ten-year-old boy or girl is as smart as she'll ever get or he'll ever get. So it's with that kind of belief I'm comfortable making the ten-year-old's insights as deep as I want."

KIDS AS INSPIRATION

In the beginning, Brian used his own children as inspiration for his writing. His first book, *Hey, Dad!*, was inspired by a diary that his daughter Megan kept on the family's cross-country holiday, at age ten. *You Can Pick Me Up at Peggy's Cove* was written for his son Ryan.

Brian jokes that after those two books he was forced to think back to his own youth for material. He has found that he remembers not only what happened when he was a kid, but also how it felt — and is able to share his keenly felt (and often hilarious) memories with his readers.

"Kids' concerns are classical concerns: Am I brave? Am I a hero? Am I honest? Do I love this person? Am I afraid? Am I admired? Am I weak? Am I strong? These are their concerns, and that's what I write about."

Writing does not always come easily, though. "When it comes, and you go unconscious while you're writing, and you stop to check and see some pages filled up, that is great. And you know that they are good because the time has gone and you haven't noticed. It's the same feeling as anything you do that you do well. You know that yourself. When you look at the clock and notice an hour has gone by, whatever you have done in that unconscious hour is good. The reverse is true as well. You write away and write away, then you look at the clock and four minutes have gone by."

DO IT YOURSELF!

Brian Doyle's book *Hey, Dad!* was based in part on the diary his daughter kept on their family vacation. Why not keep a diary of your own family holiday, and then write about some of the things that moved you?

CHRISTIANE DUCHESNE

Born: August 12, 1949, in Montreal, Quebec

Home: Montreal, Quebec

SELECTED TITLES

La Vraie Histoire du chien de Clara Vic — 1990
(Governor General's Award)

Bibitsa ou l'étrange voyage de Clara Vic — 1991
(Mr. Christie's Book Award)

Victor — 1992
(Governor General's Award)

La 42e sœur de Bébert — 1993
(Mr. Christie's Book Award)

Berthold et Lucrèce — 1995

La bergère de chevaux — 1995
(Mr. Christie's Book Award)

Who's Afraid of the Dark? — 1996

Edmond et Amandine — 1999

Le jour des monstres — 2000

When Christiane Duchesne was little, she read absolutely everything she could get her hands on. She read novels, storybooks, her parents' magazines, the dictionary — everything. And she always went to sleep with a book in her hands. Perhaps it was the diversity of this early reading material that prompted her to try so many different kinds of writing. "I think I've tried my hand at every genre, for work and also for pleasure: stories, novels, translations, songs, plays, scripts and all the writing work and research that would earn me a living."

"Everyone can make stories; it isn't just the privilege of authors."

In fact, since she began working as a writer in the mid-1970s, Christiane has translated more than four hundred titles and published more than sixty original books, seven of which she also illustrated.

For Christiane, the writing profession is ideal because it permits such a great amount of freedom — after all, how many people can do their jobs with just a pencil and a paper napkin? But Christiane wasn't always so sure of the path she would take. "I never actually decided to 'become an author.' I had always written for my own enjoyment, but I never believed that I could write for a living; the proof of which is in the fact that I went to study industrial design at an architectural college. But for whatever reason, by chance or by destiny, it was writing that got the upper hand."

And now writing is what Christiane does every day. "I never let myself get stopped by writer's block. If the ideas aren't coming, I just do something else. And since I have a million things to do, there are plenty to choose from."

A MILLION THINGS TO DO

Christiane really does seem to have a million things to do, and because she specializes in a number of different areas, each job is different. "This week, for example, I took three days to write a script for the next show at the Montreal Planetarium; I recorded a series of broadcasts on legends and music for Radio Canada; I gave an hour-long course on writing and radio, and I worked on a book I'm doing for Québec/Amérique. I also started writing a Christmas story and I worked out plans for a novel in my head."

With all of that on the go, there isn't much time for Christiane to do anything else. She has done a fair bit of travelling, though, and when she can fit it into her schedule,

Christiane enjoys talking to kids.

She recalls being invited to talk to a group of grade-two students at a local library. The group arrived with a substitute teacher who didn't seem to know anything about the visit, and it soon became obvious to Christiane that the students were getting more and more restless. After a time, one little girl stood and asked when the show was supposed to begin. Apparently, because the substitute teacher had not been specific about the kind of show they would be attending, the class assumed they were going to see marionettes or some other fabulous spectacle that Christiane could not provide. It made for an awkward visit indeed, and now she's careful to tell her audiences up front: "Listen, this may be very, very dull, but the show is me!"

This description actually isn't too far off the mark, because with

her many skills Christiane Duchesne really is a kind of one-person show!

DO IT YOURSELF!

To do Christiane Duchesne's activity, you'll need a partner. Use a dictionary to make a list of ten words each which are new to you. Then exchange papers and, without looking up the definitions of the words, write a short story using every word on your partner's list. The challenging part is making up meanings for all of those words. Share your stories, and only then look up the real definitions.

SARAH ELLIS

Born: May 19, 1952,
in Vancouver, British Columbia

Home: Vancouver, British Columbia

SELECTED TITLES

The Baby Project — 1986

Next-Door Neighbours — 1989

Putting Up with Mitchell — 1989

Pick-Up Sticks — 1991
(Governor General's Award)

Out of the Blue — 1994
(Mr. Christie's Book Award)

Back of Beyond — 1996

*The Young Writer's
Companion* — 1999

Next Stop — 2000

*A Prairie as Wide
as the Sea* — 2001

*Girls' Own: A Canadian
Anthology* (editor) — 2001

Vicky Metcalf Award winner, 1995

A childhood friend. "She said, 'I always knew you were going to be a writer,' and I asked, 'Oh, how did you know that?' She said, 'You told me so.'

"I guess I did, but I can't remember it. I wasn't one of those kids who wrote novels when I was twelve. I turned thirty and I needed a change in my life. I was a librarian; I really wanted to do something that was more independent. So I took a six-month sabbatical and jumped in. If my friend Doreen is right, I guess I always wanted to."

AN OBLIGATION TO BE AMUSING

Sarah remembers her childhood: "We had a lot of reading aloud and storytelling in my family. Lots of stories about my parents' childhood — my mom's childhood on the Prairies, and my dad's in London. And there was kind of a dinnertime thing when people said what they did in the day, and it was pretty well an obligation to be amusing. I was the youngest, so I had to get my chops in order pretty quickly so that I could hold my own."

Sarah's skill at spinning tales would naturally carry over into her writing. Here's how her new career got off the ground: "I had been sending around some manuscripts for picture books and they had all been rejected, and I got a very nice rejection letter from Groundwood Books saying, 'We can't do this picture book, but if you ever think of writing a short novel please send it to us.' I was incredibly inspired by this, so I did and they published it."

Sarah really surprised herself with this first book. *The Baby Project* was not the kind of book she had set out to try and write. She explains, "I really was intending to write a rather lighthearted chapter book for new readers, sort of like Beverly Cleary. I adore that stuff and that's what I wanted to write. But as I wrote, it got darker and darker and longer and longer and the protagonist got older so that's what it ended up being.

> *"Writing is like playing some sort of game . . . you get so into it that the world disappears and you get to be powerful and in charge."*

"Just because you want to write a certain kind of thing doesn't mean that's what's going to come out. It's always a balancing act for me between letting it happen and making it happen, because there's got to be a bit of both. You have to give yourself a bit of slack to go in another direction, but you can't just become a jellyfish."

Like every author, Sarah is often asked where her ideas come from. "The short answer is there are three places I get ideas. One is memory, two is observation — being alert to the world around you, listening to people's stories, asking questions, and gathering impressions — and the third one is dreams, because that's where all the weird stuff comes from. I'm not a fantasy writer, but still I write down my dreams and I enjoy them a lot. It's like a movie that you get to watch while you sleep. I get up first thing before they dissolve and just write them down. Not everything, though. Sometimes they're about going shopping at Safeway."

Though she's now a seasoned author, and has even written an inspiring guide for young writers, Sarah still finds that every book she writes presents new challenges. "In my fourth book, all of a sudden I realized I had no idea how to divide a book into

A Prairie as Wide as the Sea

The Immigrant Diary of Ivy Weatherall

Milorie, Saskatchewan, 1926

"...riveting tales that take readers to the edge of reality." School Library Journal (starred review)

Sarah Ellis

Back of Beyond

[stories]

chapters. Now, for the first two books, I didn't even think about that. I just would end a chapter and start a chapter. All of a sudden I thought, Well, this is pretty arbitrary. Why not a paragraph before or a paragraph after? I got self-conscious about it and all of a sudden didn't know how to do it. All of my books have thrown up this kind of unexpected thing I have to learn."

A voracious reader, Sarah still works at the library, although she's cut her time down to three days a week to devote more time to her books. She writes from a little office in the attic of her house. Beneath sloped walls, she looks directly into the property of her neighbour, a former junk dealer with a yard full of junk. "It's not picturesque," she muses, "but it is interesting!"

DO IT YOURSELF!

Sarah Ellis suggests that instead of writing about what you know, write about what you like. And if that doesn't work, she suggests you take off your shoe, put it on the table in front of you and write about that. Sometimes a little doodling is all it takes to get you going.

EUGENIE FERNANDES

Born: September 25, 1943, in Huntington, New York, USA

Home: Peterborough, Ontario

SELECTED TITLES

A Difficult Day — 1987

Just You and Me — 1993

Waves in the Bathtub — 1993

The Tree that Grew to the Moon — 1994

🎨 *How Big Is Big?* — 1999

🎨 *Ribbon Rescue* — 1999

Ordinary Amos and the Amazing Fish — 2000

📝 *Sleepy Little Mouse* — 2000

🎨 *Cappuccina Goes to Town* — 2001

One More Pet — 2001

🎨 — *illustrations only*
📝 — *text only*

The Golden Book series was started the year before Eugenie Fernandes was born, and those were the books she loved when she was growing up, reading them mostly for the art. Some years later, continuing her relationship with the series, Eugenie actually wrote and illustrated Golden Books of her own, and when they were published, she was understandably thrilled. "I got a big kick out of looking in the backs of the Golden Books because they have a list of their classics. And there I was with these illustrators that I really loved."

"I think I lived the stories when I was a child."

Eugenie began her career as an illustrator when a co-worker at the greeting card company where she was working suggested she talk to an agent. Eugenie followed this advice and soon published a story which she now describes as "just horrible." The story was called *Wicked Dishrag* and it was about a nasty little girl who dresses up like a witch for Halloween and begins to turn into one for real because she is so good at it.

"I did a lot of forgettable little cheap books, but I'm really grateful for those because I didn't come out of art school like Nicola Bayley — she is just marvellous. I had to struggle along until I got to be a little bit better."

IT HAS TO SOUND GOOD

Part of that struggle involves fine-tuning the language of her stories. "It has to sound good and not just be an interesting story; the words have to feel good in your mouth. There's a rhythm — not a rhyme — in the sentence structure. Sometimes when I'm writing I'll have a word that needs to be two syllables and the word I've written is only one syllable. So then I'll go searching around for a word with the right number of syllables in it so that it works with my cadence, my voice."

For as long as she can remember, Eugenie has loved the outdoors. As a child she lived near the beach. "In the summertime I was always up a tree or at the beach or under the water. Those were the three places you could find me."

Today, you can find Eugenie in her studio overlooking a lake. Weather permitting, she rises before the sun and sits by the water to think. Readers will recognize Eugenie's continuing fascination with water and nature popping up in such books as *Waves in the Bathtub* and *The Tree that Grew to the Moon*.

Eugenie says, "I always like to have a story in the back of my mind." She goes on to explain that she usually has two or three ideas "waiting" for her to have time to work on them. "When I go to bed at night, I think about stories and write them in my head. And by the time I have the story written — because I've done it in my head — I usually have it memorized."

Eugenie believes there are three important things to remember when you are writing a story. First and foremost, you should write what you know because a story has to have your feelings in it. "If your dog got run over, write about that. If you have a wonderful treehouse where you like to hide, write about that."

Second, there has to be some tension. "Even in a happy story like *Waves in the Bathtub*, there's a bit of tension in the mother wanting Kady to scrub her toes!"

Third, Never give up. This message came from some young fans of hers, and Eugenie says she repeats it to herself whenever she's feeling discouraged.

But it takes more than that to stay happy in this business. Eugenie says that you shouldn't write books unless you love it, "because it's very discouraging in the beginning. Before I was doing books professionally I would make books anyway — for nobody, for no reason. I was constantly writing stories and making little books. Anyone going into the business has to be quite determined and able to get up again when publishers say, Don't call us. We'll call you."

DO IT YOURSELF!

Eugenie Fernandes can look at a piece of driftwood and see a horse or a fish or a mermaid. She suggests that you find a stick or a stone and, once you've decided what it reminds you of, paint it to enhance the resemblance.

KIM FERNANDES

Born: September 4, 1969,
in Huntington, New York, USA

Home: Port Perry, Ontario

SELECTED TITLES

Visiting Granny — 1990

*Zebo and the
Dirty Planet* — 1991

🎨 *Just You and Me* — 1993

🎨 *One Grey Mouse* — 1995

*Christmas Crafts with
Crayola Model Magic* — 1997

🎨 *Little Toby and
the Big Hair* — 1997

🎨 *A Visit from St. Nicholas* — 1999

🎨 *How Big Is Big?* — 1999

🎨 *Sleepy Little Mouse* — 2000

🎨 *Busy Little Mouse* — 2001

🎨 — *illustrations only*

When Kim Fernandes's grade-thirteen art class was cancelled due to lack of enrollment, Kim asked the teacher if she could do an independent project instead. She chose clay as her medium; it was a decision that would eventually shape her career.

Kim remembers, "Even though I liked to draw and paint, it never came out the way I envisioned it. But with clay, in three dimensions, I guess I felt I had more control. I could manipulate it.

"I did three-dimensional scenes, sort of like you're looking into a little doll's house. I used wood and fabric and clay — a mixed media. Then at the end of the school year, my mom suggested writing a children's book about the house. With help from her, I came up with the story *Visiting Granny*."

Kim's mom, Eugenie Fernandes, also helped her get that all-important first meeting with a publisher, but it was by no means the first time Kim had visited Annick Press. Kim has been a regular visitor there since she was little, having accompanied her mother whenever she delivered a job. "They still call me Kimmy!" she laughs.

Kim still recalls the day she first presented her own work. She says, "I got an appointment with them and they thought my three-dimensional style was kind of unique. Of course, they had lots of work for me to do on my story, and once it was all approved, I had to work on more scenes."

> *"I've got my thumbprints in every piece of clay."*

It was at about this time that Kim Fernandes, with a grandfather and both parents professional illustrators, finally decided that she, too, would become an illustrator. "I had the art bug from birth. It was just always a part of growing up. On rainy days when my brother and I had nothing to do, we would fill it with a craft. I really didn't think about art as a career. I just assumed everybody did it. That is, until grade thirteen, when I had to buckle down. I waffled with being a marine biologist or a vet. I loved animals, but I didn't have the science credits, so I decided to be an artist."

Kim was accepted at the Ontario College of Art where she would eventually develop the skills to become what she calls "a full-time illustrator, part-time author."

Kim uses a special kind of plastic clay called Fimo, which is commonly used for making jewellery, beads and necklaces. Kim has developed her own techniques for making three-dimensional book illustrations with the medium.

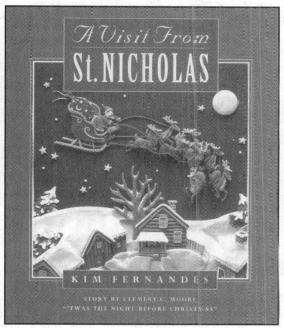

To create each of the Fimo pieces that make up her pictures, she begins by drawing a sketch on tracing paper. She then uses a hand-crank pasta machine on the "lasagna" setting to flatten her Fimo. Working on a non-stick cookie sheet, Kim positions her paper over the clay and pokes around the edges of her drawing before lifting the paper away with the tip of a knife.

That's when the real fun begins. Following her punch marks, she rounds out the edges of her pieces, sculpting in wrinkles, textures and patterns as she goes, using just about every tool imaginable — including a sewing needle for hair and a toothbrush for dirt.

It takes Kim between a week and ten days to do a picture, and when she's finally done she carefully removes any dust or hairs (her cats are very nosy) and bakes it in the oven for about half an hour. The clay hardens as it cools.

PRACTICE MAKES PERFECT

In making her unique illustrations, Kim has learned a few tricks. For instance, she's discovered that using a heavy-gauge pan will prevent her work from cracking in the heat of the oven. She's also found that an addition like a pretty tree, for instance, can cover the occasional mistake. Kim has found the ideal way to store her illustrations, as well: in pizza boxes, which she calls her "high-tech Fimo carrying cases." Each book requires about sixteen of them.

When Kim was a kid, her grandmother had a sneaky way of encouraging Kim's love of books. Kim recalls, "She would give me a quarter for every book I read. Of course, I'd have to write her a letter and a small synopsis of the story before she would send me back a quarter!"

Today Kim has found a way of focusing her own efforts. "At night, for half an hour before I go to sleep, sort of like athletes visualize the race ahead, I visualize making something out of clay. I think of the colours and of what I'm going to do first. And the next day, I'll make it."

DO IT YOURSELF!

Kim Fernandes suggests you try making your own three-dimensional picture. Start by drawing a sketch on a paper plate. Then soften some Plasticine and use your thumb to press it into your sketch, working from the background to the foreground.

SHEREE FITCH

Born: December 3, 1956,
in Ottawa, Ontario

Home: Washington, DC, USA

SELECTED TITLES

Toes in My Nose — 1987

Sleeping Dragons — 1989
all Around

*There Were Monkeys
in My Kitchen* — 1992
(Mr. Christie's Book Award)

I Am Small — 1994

Mable Murple — 1995

*If You Could Wear
My Sneakers* — 1997
(Hackmatack Award)

*There's a Mouse in
My House* — 1998

*The Jullabaloo
Bugaboo Day* — 1998

If I Were the Moon — 1999

Writing Maniac — 2000

Vicky Metcalf Award winner, 2000

Sheree Fitch published her first poem when she was in the second grade. She recalls, "I had this wonderful teacher named Mrs. Goodwin. It was a silly poem. It was not profound. It was a tongue twister. But she said, 'Yes, it's a poem, it's a nonsense poem.' And she printed it in her own printing and thumbtacked it on a felt panel in the school fair. As far as I'm concerned, that was my first publication, because I stood that day and watched parents and teachers and other students walk by and look and read my poem and smile. I remember thinking, Wow! Something I wrote could make somebody smile. It was the moment I realized how words have power — how words could affect how a person feels. For me it was a 'eureka!' moment, seeing that writing wasn't just about writing for yourself; it was about communicating with others."

Sheree sold her first short story at the age of nineteen, for forty-five dollars. She nearly didn't open the envelope, because at the time she was sure it was a rejection letter and she just couldn't bear to read it.

It was lucky that she did. She laughs when she remembers, "I went out and I bought white shower curtains with the money, and every time I went in the bathroom I would say to myself, Yes, I really am a writer. I bought those shower curtains with that money."

In Sheree's home there are bookshelves everywhere and, of course, monkeys in the kitchen, although these ones are stuffed. But that's not where Sheree got the idea for her book *There Were Monkeys in My Kitchen!* She explains, "It was a direct result of calling my own boys monkeys. They bounced their basketballs into the kitchen and I said, 'You two monkeys get those basketballs out of this kitchen this minute.' They said, 'We're not monkeys, Mom!' and I said, 'Yes, you are. There are monkeys in my kitchen.'"

Sometimes it's the smallest seed of an idea that can send Sheree off to her writing. Once when she was visiting a school, a student told her that every dinosaur's name is a poem. Sheree beams at the recollection. "I loved that because I'm always saying to students, I think each

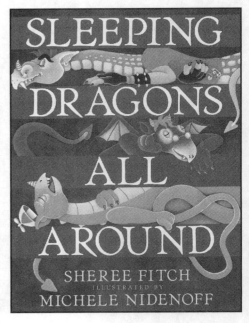

word should be a poem. You've got to look at it that way. Tomatoes, cucumbers — listen to the rhythm and the cadence of the word." That student's observation inspired her to develop the text for her book *When Dinosaurs Dine by Moonlight*.

"I truly fall in love with one word or a sound. I take words like 'giggle' and 'bagel' and 'beluga' and 'bugle' and, yes, seven years later I actually do have a poem."

SIMPLE DOES NOT EQUAL EASY

Sheree says it takes her about two years to get every word in a poem the way she wants it. She explains, "To get it in an authentic child's voice and not a contrived rhyme, and to tell a good story and not be too predictable with rhyme so that it sounds like a metronomic clip-clop, for me it's never, never easy.

"Every once in a while I have a poem and I say, Wow, that's what I've been working twenty years to get! And then, of course, I go on to the next challenge, and I've got to learn it again. I find poetry an incredibly challenging art form, whether it's for adults or for children. I'm still learning how to be a good nonsense writer."

When she's working on a new poem, Sheree likes to bounce her ideas off two of her friends who are also writers. "We're never cruel to each other," she says, "but we're honest.

"I know that there are some writers who really feel it's bad luck to talk about their work when it's in progress, for fear of talking it all out. I think there might be something to that, but I also feel there's a point in the process where I need to begin to talk to at least one or two people, because it begins to make it real to me."

When asked to describe the most unusual place she has ever found herself writing, Sheree replies, "On an iceberg in the Arctic. I was up there doing a literacy event, and we went out and climbed this iceberg. When I got to the top, I saw that people had used their fingers to write their names in the snow. For me, it was this wonderful image of graffiti."

Determined to leave her own mark, Sheree "wrote" a few lines with her finger. To this day she doesn't remember what she said, though. After climbing down from her icy perch, Sheree tried to record what she had etched in the ice, but the ink in her pen was frozen.

Text by Sheree Fitch
Illustrations by Leslie Elizabeth Watts

DO IT YOURSELF!

Sheree Fitch suggests you try this trick for coming up with a writing idea: Begin by picking a letter of the alphabet. Then, working only for a minute, write down all of the words you can think of that begin with that letter. When you're done, you could have the beginning of a tongue-twisty sentence or poem.

MARIE-LOUISE GAY

Born: June 17, 1952,
in Quebec City, Quebec

Home: Outremont, Quebec

SELECTED TITLES

Moonbeam on a Cat's Ear — 1986
(Amelia Frances Howard-Gibbon Award)

Rainy Day Magic — 1987
(Amelia Frances Howard-Gibbon Award,
Governor General's Award)

Mademoiselle Moon — 1992

Rabbit Blue — 1993

🎨 *The Fabulous Song* — 1996
(Mr. Christie's Book Award)

🎨 *The Christmas Orange* — 1998

Stella, Star of the Sea — 1999
(Mr. Christie's Book Award,
Ruth Schwartz Award)

On My Island — 2000

Stella, Queen of the Snow — 2000
(Elizabeth Mrazik-Cleaver Award)

🎨 *Yuck, A Love Story* — 2000
(Governor General's Award)

🎨 — illustrations only

As Marie-Louise Gay recalls her childhood, "I was a constant reader — we're talking five to seven books a week. My parents would take me to the library on Saturdays, and I would get a pile of books. I would go right through them, and next Saturday I was back again. I had a book in front of me all the time."

Marie-Louise started drawing professionally when she was eighteen years old. "I was an editorial illustrator and a cartoon illustrator. I had been doing illustration for at least five years when I started illustrating a few books for children. At that point, a desire came up to write my own stories because I found that I liked to be able to play around with the words and the images so they'd influence each other. When you have a set story you can't necessarily do that. It's sort of like going around with one eye closed. So I decided I would open up a bit and try writing — and it worked."

Because she was already working as an art director in a publishing house when she submitted her first story and illustrations, Marie-Louise knew all about what was involved in publishing books. "What was exciting to me was seeing people read my book for the first time and realizing that I had done something that would last and that would be read over and over again. Because before that I was a commercial illustrator. I would illustrate for magazines and stuff like that, which is really temporary. People wrap up their potato peels in your illustrations. But the impact you could have by illustrating and writing a book! It would hang around; it would go into libraries; kids would borrow it; kids would lend it to their friends. I had finally found something that was enduring."

> *"Don't copy anyone else. Draw what you see and develop your own style. Originality is the most important thing."*

Marie-Louise uses pen and ink, watercolours and dyes to do her illustrations. And even though much of what she draws appears to be fanciful, she actually does do a lot of research.

"Since my books are very whimsical, there's not a lot of normal research involved. To give you an example, when I worked on *Mademoiselle Moon*, which is highly imaginative, I did research for moon and sun words — words that would make word plays in my text. Then I looked up different ways the moon and the sun have been illustrated throughout the years in all different types of things — old encyclopedias, postcards — just to influence my drawing and my perspective of seeing the sun and the moon. If I was to show you the things I used, you wouldn't see any relationship with the way I draw, but they're reference points."

HER OWN SPECIAL STYLE

"Now, if I talk about a book like *Rainy Day Magic*, where you have the huge tiger and the whale, I went and got photographs of the animals and then I started deforming them into my style. So you have a tiger who looks like a tiger, but his paws are small and his head's very big. To me it's always really important to realize that even if I draw these strange-looking animals or people, that underneath, in my mind, they really have bones and must be able to move around. You want the book to be consistent so you'll recognize the hero or the animal throughout the book. You have to understand how the animal or the hero is made underneath."

Marie-Louise offers these pointers to young people interested in becoming authors and illustrators: "Keep your eyes open all the time. That's when you get your ideas. Look around you and see how people walk and how dogs sniff trees, how flowers look in a certain light and how people move. Listen to songs and stories being told and all of this becomes part of your identity as an author and an illustrator."

DO IT YOURSELF!

Take a tip from Marie-Louise Gay and collect some photographs of real animals. Then combine elements from each to invent an animal that doesn't exist. Draw an environment to suit your creature, and decide how it will move and what it will eat. Think carefully before you draw: If you've done an animal with an anteater snout, it couldn't be eating watermelons. Of course, if your pictures are as fanciful as Marie-Louise's, maybe it could be!

PHOEBE GILMAN

Born: April 4, 1940,
in New York City, New York, USA

Home: Toronto, Ontario

SELECTED TITLES

The Balloon Tree — 1985

Jillian Jiggs — 1985

Little Blue Ben — 1986

*The Wonderful Pigs
of Jillian Jiggs* — 1988

Grandma and the Pirates — 1990

🎨 *Once Upon
a Golden Apple* — 1991

Something from Nothing — 1992
(Ruth Schwartz Award)

Jillian Jiggs to the Rescue — 1994

The Gypsy Princess — 1995

Pirate Pearl — 1998

*Jillian Jiggs and the
Secret Surprise* — 1999

Vicky Metcalf Award winner, 1993

🎨 — *illustrations only*

"No one ever inspired me in school," Phoebe Gilman recalls. "In fact, I was the kid in the background who did what she was told, and did nothing particularly extraordinary. I was good at drawing; I was good at writing. But I wasn't the best at drawing, and I wasn't the best at writing. And I never did anything especially outstanding that a teacher would say, Wow, we have someone special in this class!"

Without encouragement, it was many years before Phoebe decided to try her hand at children's books. Inspiration came one day when, on a walk, her daughter's balloon burst on a tree branch. Phoebe imagined a magic tree blossoming in balloons and began work on her first story, *The Balloon Tree*.

Phoebe fiddled with her story for a long time, treating it as a hobby, while continuing to work as a professional artist. Finally, she sent it, and her drawings, to publisher after publisher. "I kept getting back rejection slips, but that was okay because it wasn't my 'serious work.' I was just doing it as a lark."

Gradually, though, her book became more important to her. She decided that she really liked writing and illustrating and loved picture books. And, from that point on, Phoebe wouldn't take no for an answer. "I kept getting all these rejection slips — I got over fifty rejection slips just for *The Balloon Tree*, and I was driving my family crazy because every time I'd rewrite it they'd have to listen to the newest version."

PERSISTENCE PAYS OFF

Persistence paid off, though, and in 1984, Scholastic accepted Phoebe's story. "It was months of rewriting and working back and forth, and it was a real education for me on what makes a picture-book story work. I didn't know things like it has to fit into thirty-two pages and you've got to leave enough room for pictures in those thirty-two pages. It meant considerable chopping out and editing down."

"At one point I said: Wait a minute, I love doing this. My kids had all outgrown the picture book stage and I was still going back to that part of the library. They would be mortified: 'Mom, please, we don't read those kind of books anymore!'"

Why didn't Phoebe, an illustrator by profession, think about the space she would have to leave for her pictures? "I think, at heart, I am a writer who was trained as an artist, because what

I'm always drawn to in a book are the words, not the pictures. I will buy picture books for the pictures alone to study them because they're beautiful. But the books I love, I love because of the words."

Even as a child, Phoebe was drawn to books that had no pictures at all (though she confesses to a great love of comic books). She remembers, in particular, searching for good books about adventurous girls. "I read the Nancy Drew series mainly because there were so few books with female heroines — at least Nancy Drew was a hero, of sorts. With all the other books — even the fairy tales — you had to do a kind of mental flip-flop to make yourself into the male hero." One can't help but wonder if this is the reason Phoebe decided to make her most-loved character, Jillian, a girl.

But that wasn't the real reason Jillian came to be. After her first book was published, Phoebe began to look for ideas for her second book. "I went back to the portfolio I had done when

I was looking for work — I had done a lot of samples just using Mother Goose rhymes. One of the Mother Goose rhymes I had used was 'Gregory Griggs.' 'Gregory, Gregory, Gregory Griggs, / Wore twenty-seven different wigs . . . ' is the way the rhyme goes, and I had a picture of a little boy with a mop on his head who was turning everything in the house into a wig. I thought he looked like a girl, so I decided to change him into one. I looked for a three-syllable girl's name to go with Griggs and all I could come up with was Gillian, spelled with a 'G'. I dropped the 'r' from Griggs, and once Gillian was there, it just took off on its own. We changed the Gs to Js because everybody mispronounced it: Gillian Giggs."

Phoebe continues to find ideas everywhere, but she does occasionally go blank. "If I'm having trouble writing or drawing, I try not to run away from it too much, because I find it's the act of writing or the act of drawing that eventually leads me back on track. Running away is dangerous to do, because if you say, I can't work today, and you don't too often, you never work."

Do It Yourself!

Many of Phoebe Gilman's books feature heroes and villains. Make a wanted poster for the villain in your favourite book. Draw a picture of the villain, and underneath it describe his or her crime, the planned punishment and the reward for his or her capture.

LINDA GRANFIELD

Born: November 22, 1950,
in Melrose, Massachusetts, USA

Home: Etobicoke, Ontario

SELECTED TITLES

Cowboy: A Kid's Album — 1993
(Information Book Award)

*Extra! Extra!: The Who, What,
When, Where, and Why
of Newspapers* — 1993

In Flanders Fields — 1995
(Information Book Award,
Red Cedar Award)

Amazing Grace — 1997

*Silent Night:
The Song from Heaven* — 1997

Circus — 1997

*High Flight: A Story of
World War II* — 1999

Pier 21: Gateway of Hope — 2000

*Where Poppies Grow:
A World War I Companion* — 2001

*Climbing Up: Immigrant Life at
97 Orchard St., NYC* — 2001

Vicky Metcalf Award winner, 2001

Linda Granfield grew up in a family of readers. She got her first library card at the age of four. Linda remembers, "I don't know how she did it, but my mother would take some of her few extra dollars and would manage to buy us Golden Books at the grocery store when we were with her. She would hide them in her dresser drawer and when she came to read at night you'd wait to hear if she went in her room. If you heard the noise of the drawer — which I can still hear — you knew that there was a new story coming."

In those years, Linda read a great many books, but Louisa May Alcott's book *Little Women* was special. Linda read it in grade five, and she calls it "the book that changed things."

She says, "I read it and that was it: I wanted to be Jo March. That's when I got interested in writing. I made a play of *Little Women* for my classmates. I was too chicken to get up and perform so I got my friends to do the performance."

A SECONDHAND TYPEWRITER

There wasn't a lot of money when she was growing up, but Linda — the oldest of seven children — says her parents always encouraged each child's interests. When Linda showed an interest in writing, her father got her a secondhand portable typewriter.

Then in high school, Linda was asked to be the high-school reporter for the city paper. She laughs when she remembers, "I thought that sounded great. Plus I could get a pass to get out of classes! And then they said what the assignment was: 'We want you to list the menu for the high-school cafeteria each week.' For some reason, they had to print this under the high-school news in the city paper."

> *"It's the most
> exasperating craft,
> but you can't pull
> yourself away from it."*

And while writing things like "Monday: macaroni and cheese" may not have been glamorous, it did get Linda's name in print and it did provide her with an opportunity to visit the printing company in town.

She recalls, "They still had all the Linotype [typesetting] machines and you could watch the guys, with the metal type flying into the trays. They smelled like ink and they still had visors on. It was beautiful — all gone now — but it made you fall in love with words and printing and the whole process. They had creaky wooden floors and ink everywhere. It was great."

TIME TO WRITE FOR HERSELF

As an adult, Linda was interviewing authors for *Quill &*

Quire, a book-trade magazine, when someone asked her when she was going to stop writing about everyone else and start writing for herself. She took the suggestion to heart. Four years later (the printing delayed by a paper shortage and labour strike), Linda's first book, *All About Niagara Falls*, was published.

In the early years of her writing career, Linda worked in her unfinished concrete-block basement, which would get very cold. For *Cowboy: A Kid's Album*, she actually typed with fingerless gloves and bundled up in an afghan to stay warm.

Working conditions have improved considerably since then. In her finished-basement office, Linda's new challenge is a lack of space, because she collects and keeps just about everything. Linda explains, "Whatever comes through the door gets checked to see if it gets filed someplace. Real-estate ads . . . things that give prices of today, home-decorating magazines . . . "

She knows that years from now all of her thousands of books and countless bits and pieces of

paper will make rare and valuable reference tools. Halloween flyers, for instance, will remind her of the film and TV characters, snack foods and toys that were trendy in a certain year.

Linda refers to her extensive collection as she works on her own books, but other writer-friends of hers use it too — non-fiction writers as they work on specific topics, fiction writers as they attempt to create a credible setting for their stories.

Linda suggests that writers look at research as a kind of detective work. A good writer looks for clues all of the time — even while watching TV. She recommends jotting down information and ideas that catch your interest as you flip through channels. You never know when your notes will come in handy — but if you're anything like Linda, those flashes of curiosity will pay off in the long run.

DO IT YOURSELF!

When you're looking for something to write about, Linda Granfield suggests you pull an object out of the junk drawer in your house and find out everything you can about it. Ask yourself questions like, What is it made of? Where was it made? (This information might be on the wrapper or stamped somewhere on the object.) Where and why was this invented? How many are made every year? Every day? Every minute?

Linda Granfield • illustrated by Janet Wilson

BARBARA GREENWOOD

Born: September 14, 1940,
in Toronto, Ontario

Home: Toronto, Ontario

SELECTED TITLES

A Question of Loyalty — 1984

Spy in the Shadows — 1990

The Other Side of the Story — 1990

A Pioneer Story — 1994
(Information Book Award,
Mr. Christie's Book Award,
Ruth Schwartz Award)

Speak Up! Speak Out! — 1994

Pioneer Crafts — 1997

The Kids Book of Canada — 1997

The Last Safe House — 1998
(Information Book Award)

A Pioneer Thanksgiving — 1999

When Barbara Greenwood went to school, fiction writing was not part of the writing program. Instead students were expected to memorize long pieces of poetry. She laughs, "But I always thought of myself as a writer in secret!"

An avid reader, Barbara remembers spending long hours at the library, working her way through subjects that interested her. And although she read all sorts of books as a student, historical fiction was a favourite even then.

Barbara began writing in earnest when she was ten, but it wasn't until grade eleven — when a teacher cited Barbara's stories as a positive example to the rest of the class — that she began to think writing needn't be so secret an ambition after all.

Most of Barbara's books are set in Canada, a fact this author cares a great deal about. It all began when an aunt sent Barbara a copy of Lyn Cook's book *The Bells on Finland Street*. After having read so many books set in the United States, Great Britain and other unfamiliar countries, it was a startling idea to Barbara that a book could be set in Canada, in a town so close to her own home.

In her teens, the desire to write about Canadian places and events, coupled with her love for historical fiction, spurred Barbara to learn all she could about the Riel Rebellions. Researching and writing on her own time, Barbara published a piece in the high-school yearbook, which years later would become her much-acclaimed novel *A Question of Loyalty*.

> **"My mission was to do the kind of book I liked, only about where I lived."**

A WORKING SCHEDULE

For Barbara, there is no such thing as an "average" workday. She often visits schools or has other daytime errands and works at night. She does try to keep to a schedule, though, by working for three-and-a-half hours in the morning, beginning by looking at the previous night's revisions to "get primed." In the afternoons, Barbara reads the morning's writing aloud, which she believes helps her to hear the story the way the reader will hear it. In doing this she sometimes decides, for instance, that she has given one character too much to say. Barbara then makes revision notes on her printout and leaves them for the following morning, when she can begin her writing process all over again.

Barbara likes to write in chunks, completing only a few pages each day and maybe a chapter every couple of weeks. She says she must edit as she goes, all the while keeping a notebook of ideas for upcoming chapters that occur to her as she is writing. Notetaking is critical, because as Barbara says, "Those flashes come to you and go just like snow in summer."

She adds, "Ideas are everywhere, but they aren't as important as the questions you ask yourself, using the idea as a starting point. The kind of book I do starts completely with research."

When Barbara sets out to do a book, she first reads a general book on a period in history in search of the germ of a story. Then, when she finds one, she looks for first-person accounts in historical documents and old journals to expand the idea. She photocopies pages of interest from everywhere and collects them in binders, highlighting specific sections and jotting notes in the margins. She sorts her collections by category for

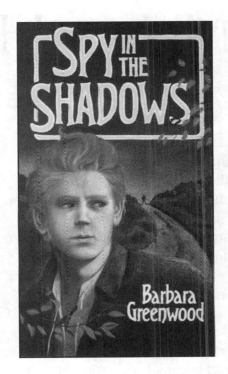

the time when she will come to use them.

Barbara doesn't gather only hard facts, however. Emotions being universal, she says, a good writer collects responses to events, and uses these remembrances in stories.

Every writer has an individual working style. Barbara says of hers, "I cannot work on more than one project at a time. My mind just doesn't work that way . . . And sometimes I don't feel like a writer at all between books, because of natural time lag. Every book is hard work. It doesn't get any easier, but it's worthwhile. It's in the struggle that the ideas come up."

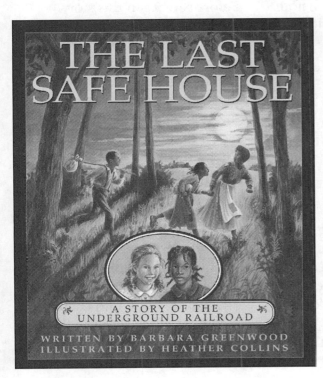

DO IT YOURSELF!

The verb is the most powerful word in a sentence. It expresses not just the action, but also the emotion. Barbara Greenwood suggests that you use the best verbs you can find. She also suggests you plunge into the action of your story without spending too much time describing things. Get the reader's attention, and keep it, with action.

MONICA HUGHES

Born: November 3, 1925,
in Liverpool, England

Home: Edmonton, Alberta

SELECTED TITLES

Gold-Fever Trail — 1974

The Keeper of the Isis Light — 1980

The Guardian of Isis — 1981
(Canada Council Prize)

Hunter in the Dark — 1982
(Canada Council Prize,
CLA Young Adult Book Award)

Little Fingerling — 1989

The Crystal Drop — 1992

A Handful of Seeds — 1993

The Golden Aquarians — 1994

The Other Place — 1999

Storm Warning — 2000

Vicky Metcalf Award winner, 1981

Monica Hughes's favourite place to read when she was a child was at the top of the stairs beneath a skylight, "totally away from all adult interference and supervision." Her favourite authors were Arthur Ransome and E. Nesbit.

The decision to become a writer herself came early for Monica. "At the age of about ten, I decided I was going to be a novel writer when I grew up. I went out and spent all of my pocket money on a hard-backed blank book, and I put an absolutely wonderful title on the front. Then I wrote 'Chapter One' inside, and I waited for something to happen. It didn't." Monica says she used up several other manuscript books in this way, writing only titles and the words "Chapter One," before she finally managed to write her first stories.

> *"It doesn't do any good to hit the front of your head and say, Give me an idea!"*

Now, Monica finds ideas everywhere, and she writes them all down as soon as they come to her, before they vanish, keeping them in a file marked "Ideas." And any time she's stuck for something to write about, she'll go to that file and get all the ideas out and think about them.

Ever since she received a CD player for Christmas, Monica has been listening to music while she writes. "I have found that working with music that has no interruptions — the radio doesn't work — is absolutely wonderful. If I'm writing a new book, I'll pick a piece of music that I think is going to be appropriate and that's what I play every single day."

Monica does a lot of research before she writes a book because she believes it's important to have what she calls "a really solid sense of place." In her book *The Crystal Drop*, which is set sometime in the future in southern Alberta, Monica tells the story of a journey by two young people from the farm where they've been living to their uncle's place in the foothills. Before she began this story, Monica stayed in Lethbridge for a week. She visited Head-Smashed-In Buffalo Jump, and as she walked through the rooms of the museum, she described what she saw while talking into a tape recorder. She also interviewed one of the archeologists while she was there. Then she drove along the back roads that her characters would have travelled and noted the scenery and her car's odometer readings. Finally, she marked her characters' route on a big topographical map, then divided her book into chapters according to the distance the kids in her story would have been able to travel on foot.

After her research is finished, writing the first draft of a story isn't a long process for Monica. She writes between nine and twelve o'clock every morning, usually completing about two thousand words at each sitting to finish a chapter in two days.

If she isn't sure about spelling or punctuation, she doesn't worry about looking it up right away. Instead Monica marks it with a wiggly line and checks it later, after she's finished her thought. When the first draft is complete, Monica puts her text into her computer and prints off a copy on which she uses a red pen to do her revisions. Monica then puts her manuscript aside for a time, so that when she reads it again she does so like a stranger. It helps her to look at her work objectively.

When asked if she had any tips for young writers, Monica said, "Keep a journal." She

reminds readers that a journal is not the same thing as a diary, where you're forced to put something down every day. A journal is a blank book where you put down your thoughts and your feelings. Says Monica, "It gets you in the habit of opening up." Monica also encourages kids to keep an ideas file and never give up!

DO IT YOURSELF!

Often, in Monica Hughes's books, characters with very different backgrounds share an adventure. She suggests that you and your friends clip a collection of human interest stories out of the newspaper. Then mix the clippings up, select two at random and write a story that ties the two together.

Where the two ideas intersect, the story begins.

BERNICE THURMAN HUNTER

Born: November 3, 1922,
in Toronto, Ontario

Home: Scarborough, Ontario

SELECTED TITLES

That Scatterbrain Booky — 1981

A Place for Margaret — 1984

Lamplighter — 1987

Margaret on her Way — 1988

Hawk and Stretch — 1993

Amy's Promise — 1995
(Red Cedar Award)

Janey's Choice — 1997

Two Much Alike — 1999

Booky: A Trilogy — 1998

The Runaway — 2001

Vicky Metcalf Award winner, 1990

Bernice Thurman Hunter has always enjoyed reading realistic stories, so it follows that she would prefer writing realistic stories as well. But this particular kind of story requires a fair bit of research, so Bernice is always on the lookout for ideas.

"All of my books are based on real people. The Booky books are almost autobiographical — except that my brother says that that's not the way it happened. My family argues about that, and I just tell them to write their own book because I'm writing my memories."

Bernice remembers particularly fondly the time she had the honour of meeting one of her favourite authors. "I met L.M. Montgomery when I was fourteen years old — I idolized her, of course — and actually had tea with her in her back garden. I describe that event in *As Ever, Booky*; it's practically word for word what happened."

When she's not writing about her own life experiences, Bernice looks to other sources. One quest for a short-story idea came to an end when she was standing in a department store line-up. "I heard these two women in front of me talking, so I just eavesdropped. They were talking about when they were kids; how they'd had this terrible fight and how they had resolved it. It was such a good idea that I just ran right home and wrote the story."

She also recalls with some embarrassment that, before she could escape, the little boy who was with the women turned around and said to his mother, "That nosy old lady's listening!" Bernice was caught in the act, but she was convinced it was worth it — and so was her publisher.

THE RISKS OF BEING A WRITER

In fact, Bernice learned from an early age that embarrassment isn't the only thing a writer is likely to suffer in search of a great story. When she was a girl, Bernice carefully put together her own newspaper. She made copies by hand, then passed them around the neighbourhood. "I thought I was a writer then."

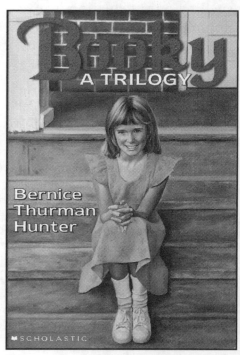

But not everyone appreciated the effort that went into that first publication. Bernice recalls, "I remember I reported news on the kids and what they were up to. I had some boys beat me up after school because I put in some mischief they had gotten into!"

"I like writing the type of stories that I like reading, which are real stories. I guess I'm just what you'd call a realist."

Years later, Bernice had a more positive newspaper experience; it was the first time she had ever published a piece for money. As a guest writer for *The Toronto Star*, Bernice wrote an article entitled "A Grandchild Can Make Life Beautiful Again" and received fifty dollars for her effort. Although she had published other articles, that first cheque made her feel like a real author. She remembers receiving a letter from the paper's regular columnist, encouraging her to keep at it. "Seeing those words from another successful writer gave me the courage to keep on writing, which I did."

Over the years, Bernice's books have been appreciated by readers from eight to eighty. She recalls one particularly enthusiastic reader who sent her a list of her books, beside which he had written how often he had reread each — some as many as ten or fifteen times!

Bernice welcomes the opportunity to motivate young readers. Every year she does a special Booky tour with a lucky group of schoolchildren in Scarborough, Ontario. After everyone is familiar with the Booky books, they board a bus and visit all of the places described in the series. Perhaps Bernice is thinking back to her own school days, when she herself was encouraged by a special grade-eight teacher named Mr. Johnston. "He always liked my stories, and because at that time I didn't have the nerve to stand up and talk in front of people — my legs would actually shake — he would read the stories to the class for me. That's what I call encouragement!"

Do It Yourself!

Bernice Thurman Hunter suggests you write about yourself. Think about an important or memorable thing that has happened to you, then start writing.

JULIE JOHNSTON

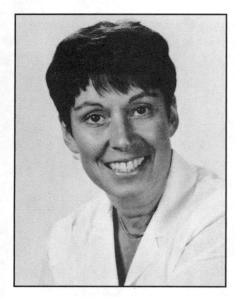

Born: January 21, 1941,
in Smiths Falls, Ontario

Home: Peterborough, Ontario

SELECTED TITLES

Hero of Lesser Causes — 1992
(Governor General's Award)

Adam and Eve and Pinch-me — 1994
(CLA Young Adult Book Award,
Governor General's Award,
Ruth Schwartz Award)

The Only Outcast — 1998

Love Ya Like a Sister — 1999

In Spite of Killer Bees — 2001

Growing up as the middle sister in a family of three girls, Julie Johnston spent a lot of time reading as a child — horse books, especially, and all of L.M. Montgomery's Anne novels. But the fictional character she felt closest to was Louisa May Alcott's struggling writer, Jo March.

Julie says, "I wanted to be a writer for a long time. In high school I did a lot of writing — I did it for the yearbook and the school paper, and I wrote plays for our class to put on. I thought then that I wanted to be a writer, and my plan was that I would go into journalism, because I didn't know how else you became a writer."

As time went by, however, Julie was swayed by what she calls "the power of love." She followed her boyfriend — who is now her husband — to the University of Toronto, where there was no course in journalism. Julie laughs when she recalls what she did study: "Occupational therapy!"

But the writing bug remained. Years later, when her oldest daughter complained of never getting a good part in the school play, Julie began writing plays for all four of her children. She recalls, "They'd put them on for their relatives, or they'd get their friends in and we'd have sort of neighbourhood plays and all the parents would come and watch. It was fun. It really was."

Eventually, Julie decided to go back to school to study drama and try her hand at writing what she calls "a real play." She entered her work *There's Going to Be a Frost* in a Canadian playwriting competition and, to her delight, it won first prize. Six months later, *Chatelaine* magazine published one of her short stories, and in Julie's own words, "That's when I thought, I can do this!"

But even with that confident beginning, it took Julie six years and about seven revisions to find a publisher for her first novel. "I had a long period of time when everything was pointing away from writing. It was a very frustrating time."

Many years later, Julie says she's still learning about writing, but she has developed a better understanding of the process. Julie explains, "I have to get most

of the work done early on, then I can relax. There is a last-minute element to it, because I do a lot of changing at the very end when I think, This isn't what I wanted to say at all."

Julie says her characters never take over and dictate where the story will go. "I kind of hate that concept. Some people say, 'Oh, the book wrote itself.' Well this never happens to me. I'm always in there slugging away trying to write the darn thing. [But] characters do take on a life. They become more colourful as you work with them."

"I like to be as true to life as possible."

For her book *Love Ya Like a Sister*, Julie found herself not creating characters, but writing about real people. After a teenaged girl died unexpectedly on a family vacation in Paris, her mother decided to publish the real e-mail messages her daughter had been sharing with friends back in Canada. Julie was asked to join the letters together and create a novel that would be a fitting tribute to the girl and her writing.

Julie remembers, "I went to Calgary to talk to Katie's mother and her sister and her friends. And I taped our conversations, because I knew I had to put some bridging work in, and I wanted it to be as authentic and as much in the voices of those people as I could possibly make it. The tapes were very helpful to get the way they talked and the tenor of their speech."

When asked if she has any pet peeves about being a writer, Julie replies, "I'd like to have more time to be able to write, but being an author also means you have to get out there and talk to people and read to people. I'm not a performer, so I find that very hard. I think today people expect writers to have big personalities and to be able to put on quite a little show. They want to be entertained, and I'm not able to do that."

Julie writes in a home study, a "largish" room painted a passionate shade of deep salmon. She describes it as having books and clutter everywhere, so much so that she can hardly see her desk. She has two computers — one that doesn't work and one that does — and a bulletin board covered in things she wants to remember.

In the summertime, when she isn't in her study, you may well find Julie at her family cottage on Big Rideau Lake with her dog and cat and "three leaky old boats."

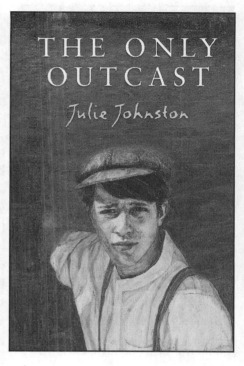

THE ONLY OUTCAST

Julie Johnston

DO IT YOURSELF!

Julie Johnston says, "I think sometimes it's difficult to write realistic dialogue, because you have to have a good ear and you almost have to be an eavesdropper. Listen to the way people talk. Listen to the rhythm of their sentences and then, once you've written it down, you should read it out loud to see if it sounds like real speech."

RUKHSANA KHAN

Born: March 13, 1962,
in Lahore, Pakistan

Home: Scarborough, Ontario

SELECTED TITLES

Bedtime Ba-a-a-lk — 1998

The Roses in My Carpets — 1998

Muslim Child — 1999

*Dahling, If You Luv Me Would You
Please, Please Smile* — 1999

King of the Skies — 2000

Rukhsana Khan never really thought about becoming a writer until her grade-eight teacher complimented her on her journal writing. She says, "I thought I couldn't be a writer because of my ethnic background, but his just saying that . . . The next year I started working on a novel. It was basically my three favourite stories all mushed together. It was called 'Carla the Gypsy Girl,' and I got to about 276 pages of adventure before I ran out of things for her to do and I gave up. But I really enjoyed it.

"Then, when I was sixteen, I wrote a little picture book called 'Waldo the Worm.' My mother was working as a cleaning lady for an English professor, and she told him about my little book. He asked to take a look at it and . . . sent it off to a friend of his. Eventually I got a rejection letter. I was really disappointed because I couldn't imagine them turning it down." Further rejection followed, and Rukhsana put her writing aside to start a family and finish school.

Years later, it would be a piece of furniture that got Rukhsana writing again. "In 1989, my husband bought me a desk . . . I was transferring my files and I came across that old rejection letter for 'Waldo the Worm' and I thought, Hey, they were encouraging me. So I rewrote 'Waldo' and I sent it off again. Then I sat back and waited for the cheque, because I really thought that's all it took."

Several rejection letters later, Rukhsana's local librarian referred her to The Canadian Children's Book Centre to find out more about becoming an author. Rukhsana recalls, "That's when I started to realize how little I knew. I thought, I'll give it a year and if in a year I don't get published, I'll just go back to being sensible about it. But along the way I fell in love with the process."

It would be more than seven years before her story *Bedtime Ba-a-a-lk* would be published.

A LENGTHY PROCESS

Before she begins writing, Rukhsana usually knows what her story's outcome will be. But as she writes, she needs to take the time to let the story evolve, as one idea gives rise to the next. Rukhsana explains, "It takes me a long time. I wish there was a faster process

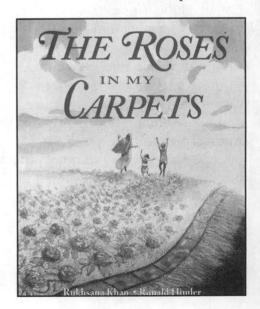

but there just isn't. Any time you try to delve deeper into the issues, it takes longer to write."

It took Rukhsana four years to write her forty-six-thousand-word novel *Dahling, If You Luv Me, Would You Please, Please Smile. The Roses in My Carpets*, at only one thousand words, took her just as long to write. And it was the wordier of the two that was the easier book to write, because of its contemporary setting and familiar content.

"It's almost like you're at the edge of a cliff and the story lies beyond. You have to make that leap of faith, and you have to hope that the story's going to catch you — and if it's not the story that you planned, it might be another one and a better one."

The Roses in My Carpets had an interesting origin. In 1992, while Rukhsana was visiting her foster child in Afghanistan, a refugee worker told her, "I want you to promise me one thing. When you go back to Canada, I want you to write something about these kids to tell people what they're going through."

Rukhsana returned home and wrote what she thought would be a magazine piece about her visit, but she couldn't get it accepted

anywhere. She wrote it and rewrote it, and then she showed it to a trusted friend. "She just looked at it and said to me, 'I don't know, Roxy. It's dead.' And I thought, Oh, my gosh, she's right, because it's all about me — and who cares about me? Maybe I have to get into his point of view.

"I thought, Okay. This boy wants to be a carpet weaver. (I don't know if my foster child wanted to be one, but that's the kind of creative licence you can take when you're writing.) I was thinking about what he must have gone through, and I was looking back over the photographs I had taken. There was one that stuck out that I hadn't noticed before. In this photograph, the boy's older brother is sitting at the back of the picture. He's got his knees drawn up, and he's got this look on his face — this look of terror — and I thought, Maybe *he's* the story and not my foster child at all."

Then one day, during an aerobics class, Rukhsana noticed a woman exercising on a floral rug. "And I thought, Okay, maybe the carpet he weaves has flowers — roses — and maybe the colours mean something to him …"

She recalls, "When I was done [writing] I was trembling and I thought, My gosh, this is good."

A student once asked Rukhsana why she allowed one of her characters to say racist things. She replied, "Sometimes your characters do things and say things that you don't approve of, but you have to let it go, because it's their point of view. If I'm going to do my job, I have to let characters say what they want."

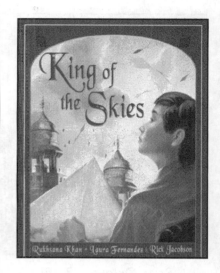

Do It Yourself!

If you want to write a well-constructed story, Rukhsana Khan suggests you think of it like a house. The beginning of a story is the foundation or basement, the middle is the walls and the ending is the roof. Each part plays an important role and, just as with a house, if any part is unsound, the story just won't hold up.

GORDON KORMAN

Born: October 23, 1963,
in Montreal, Quebec

Home: Long Island, New York,
USA; Toronto, Ontario

SELECTED TITLES

*This Can't Be Happening at
Macdonald Hall* — 1978

The Zucchini Warriors — 1988

Losing Joe's Place — 1990

The Toilet Paper Tigers — 1993

The Chicken Doesn't Skate — 1996

Liar, Liar, Pants on Fire — 1997

*The 6th Grade Nickname
Game* — 1999

The Stars from Mars — 1999

No More Dead Dogs — 2000

The Island series — 2001

Almost everyone has heard about Gordon Korman's surprise seventh-grade leap into publishing, but for those of you who haven't:
"I'm running around to schools apologizing for the seventh-grade story, but the fact is I can't leave it out. . . . Basically what happened was we had four months to work on the same project and I wrote *This Can't Be Happening at Macdonald Hall*. At the time, I was the class monitor for Arrow and TAB book clubs, so I felt this corporate responsibility towards Scholastic — although, strangely, they didn't know about me! I sent it in to the address on the book-club sheet, and I guess it went to an editor. I got really lucky. I think there was a lot of right place and right time involved."

> *"When you're writing, you're always rewriting."*

The publishing process was not all glamour for Gordon when his first book was published. "I was thrilled with the way it came out. But you have to remember what it's like to be a preteen. From the day I signed that contract to the day it came out, we're looking at close to a year and a half. I expect it to take that long now, but that was forever for me then. By the time the book came out I was practically sick of it."

Even today, Gordon admits that he's usually tired of each new book as it's finished. "I certainly have read it upside down and underwater a million times by the time it comes out. I think the difference now is that I've always got something else going. I'm always writing a new book while the one prior to it is going through editing, and the one before that is in galleys. I always have a number of things happening, so I'm never really conscious of the wait like I was before."

CRAZY HOURS

When he was first starting out, Gordon spent a great deal of time on his writing. "When I was fourteen and fifteen, writing some of those older books like *Go Jump in the Pool* and *Beware the Fish*, I would say I did the bulk of my best work in the middle of the night. I wouldn't start until eleven and worked through till three AM." Gordon says he kept these crazy hours only in the summertime, which is when he did most of his writing while he was still in school. Nowadays he does far more work during the day and in the evenings.

Life experiences do find their way into Gordon's writing, but they are never the main story line. "They're more support stuff. The school in *Son of Interflux* was an arts high school, and I wrote it

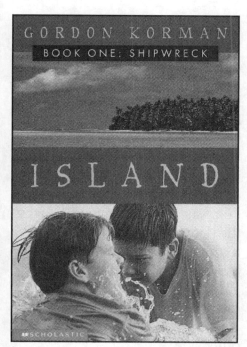

while I was in the School of the Arts in NYU. I took the college kids I knew and scaled them down four years to be in high school and wrote about my friends."

Gordon's book *The Toilet Paper Tigers* was also inspired by something that happened in his own life. "*The Toilet Paper Tigers* is about baseball and the idea started when I'd written about hockey in the Bruno and Boots books and I'd written about football in *Zucchini Warriors* and my friends were saying 'When are you going to write a baseball book?' I really didn't want to write one, so to shut them up I said, 'Tell you what, if the Blue Jays ever win the World Series, I'll write a baseball book.' I didn't think they were actually going to do it — let alone twice!"

Gordon loves his work as a writer, but he also loves the opportunities for travel that his writing affords him. "I really enjoy seeing other places and

getting around. On the other hand, sometimes that's a negative part because it doesn't give you a whole lot of continuity to your life when you're moving around so much."

Everywhere Gordon goes, he collects remarkable and surprising pieces of information. For example, at one school he visited in his travels, a student assured him that it is indeed possible to suck M&Ms through a tuba — a tidbit that found its way into one of Gordon's books. "I never run out of ideas completely. I always have a lot of things in my mind, so it's really more a question of picking which one to write about."

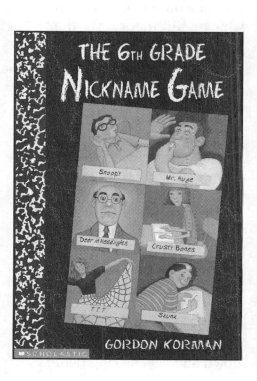

DO IT YOURSELF!

Gordon Korman's books are full of hilarious circumstances. Try this: Write down a list of characters, then a list of activities. Now match each character to the activity he or she is least likely to do in real life, and write about it. How about a baby teaching social studies, or a hockey player directing traffic? What would happen if a farmer sang opera, or a sheepdog flew a plane?

MARYANN KOVALSKI

Born: June 4, 1951,
in New York City, New York, USA

Home: Toronto, Ontario

SELECTED TITLES

Brenda and Edward — 1984

🎨 *The Cake that
Mack Ate* — 1986

🎨 *The Big Storm* — 1992

*Take Me Out to
the Ballgame* — 1993

🎨 *I Went to the Zoo* — 1993

🎨 *Doctor Knickerbocker
and Other Rhymes* — 1993

🎨 *Mable Murple* — 1995

🎨 *Princess Prunella and the Purple
Peanut* — 1996

Queen Nadine — 1998

Omar on Ice — 1999

🎨 — *illustrations only*

Maryann Kovalski grew up in New York City, where she remembers spending one special evening alone at the library, gazing at the pages of a Babar book. "Being from the Bronx, you couldn't get a place more exotic than the south of France. I was completely absorbed in the book, and when I looked up, I realized it was nightfall. Now, I have three brothers — who had obviously been looking for me in the street — and I remember going home and seeing each of them come running towards me saying, 'You're in trouble!'" That's the danger of reading!

Even though she was an insatiable reader, Maryann always knew she wanted to be an artist. However, she confesses that for a time she didn't know exactly what an illustrator was. "In my high school we would just take old pictures and copy them, so I didn't really know about any practical way that art could be applied."

When she attended art school, Maryann soon learned that illustrators were the people who drew the pictures for magazines, newspapers and picture books. Soon after graduation, she moved to Canada and was approached by Kids Can Press to do her first book for kids. After that, there was no stopping her.

"I find I can really go full steam ahead on illustrations. I sit down and get cracking right away.

It's something I can do for six hours straight." Writing, however, is considerably harder for her.

"When I'm getting stuck, I find it's best to just write. Just write anything. Write badly. People who don't succeed at things are usually the people who stop when they're in the doing-it-badly stage. They're not going to push through that great mountain of bad work to get the little spoonful of good work which is waiting for them on the other side.

> *"You have to do something badly before you're going to do it well."*

"I also keep a journal. I try to write every day, and sometimes I even write ten pages. They might be reminiscences; they might be things that are happening in my life; or sometimes I might be working out a problem."

KEEP YOUR EYES OPEN

When Maryann needs ideas for her paintings, she believes that walking and looking are very important. "I used to run off to the library's picture collection to find out things like what a building looked like, but with *The Wheels on the Bus*, I found that just standing on a street corner helped me get that feeling of a winter evening at five-thirty, when lots of people are rushing around and there's a carnival-like colour to the lights. I just kept looking and looking, and it all went into my head and into my hand, then out onto the paper."

Maryann confesses that it's sometimes hard for her to agree on the revisions her editor suggests. "Occasionally, I have moments where I say, This is good. But a lot of times you don't know what's going to work until the book's been published and reviewed. Then six months later you pick it up and say, That was pretty good, or, Ooh, that really didn't work."

To help her through the tough revision process, Maryann uses what she calls the "three times rule." "If you're showing something to someone and they make a criticism or they're confused about something, and it comes up three times, you know that something's not working."

Maryann tells children not to worry so much about being

professionals: "Savour this time of your life when you can draw what you like when you like, and don't worry so much about getting praise or criticism. I think that's really important because when you hope for recognition, you second-guess yourself and it takes away from the sheer pleasure of it."

Do It Yourself!

Do you have a job baby-sitting, raking leaves, selling lemonade or just helping around the house? Maryann Kovalski suggests you do what professional illustrators do. Make yourself a logo and advertise! A logo is a symbol or a design that represents your business name. Experiment by making different versions of your ad until you create the one that says "you."

Brenda and Edward

Maryann Kovalski

PAUL KROPP

Born: February 22, 1948,
in Buffalo, New York, USA

Home: Toronto, Ontario

SELECTED TITLES

Amy's Wish — 1984

Getting Even — 1986

Cottage Crazy — 1988

Moonkid and Liberty — 1988

The Rock — 1989

You've Seen Enough — 1991

Ellen/Eléna/Luna — 1992

Moonkid and Prometheus — 1997

System Crash — 1998

The Countess and Me — 2002

Paul Kropp made his career choice when he was still a kid. "For many years, I wanted to be a fireman, of course, and then, under the influence of two early television shows, *Perry Mason* and *The Defenders*, I decided to become a lawyer. Had I been smart, I would have stayed with that, because almost all of my friends have become lawyers and they're much wealthier than I am. But I decided to become a writer in grade six, thanks to my principal, a fellow named Alfred J. Labiak, who was the subject of a feature piece in the first underground newspaper to be produced at Public School 81. The underground newspaper was produced on my typewriter because I was the one who had a typewriter.

"Mr. Labiak had the paper in his hands within three days and called me into the office and said, 'Kropp, did you do this?' I said yes and I was punished. That was when I learned that writing has power."

Paul Kropp was teaching at a vocational school when he decided to write his first novel. He wanted to write something for the kids who didn't enjoy reading, and put together the first few pages of what eventually became *Burn Out*. Then, he went looking for publishers. "I went alphabetically, starting with the As. I got as far as the Cs." After Collier Macmillan agreed to sign

him up, Paul says, "I was so thrilled I almost forgot to ask them to pay me anything."

IDEAS FROM REAL LIFE

Paul always gets his ideas from real life. He explains, "I have a limited imagination. I almost invariably draw characters from either a school that I visit or a school where I teach."

Although his writing no longer permits him to teach full time, Paul continues to teach a creative writing course at the high-school level. He says it helps him to stay current and, of course, allows him to find models for the characters in his books.

He also finds that because his students are comfortable working

with him, they aren't afraid to tell him what they think about his books. "My creative writing class felt no bones about saying, 'Boy, why don't you cut the first page of this new book of yours and start with page two?' And I imagine they were right. I've done that, anyhow, so I hope they're right!"

> "If you haven't read two thousand books by the time you're twenty, you haven't read enough."

In addition to working directly with the students who will eventually be reading his books, Paul prepares in other ways. "My work requires a great deal of research. I've never been in a gang. I've never smoked dope. I've never been a woman. I've never been on a horse. I've never ridden a motorcycle. I've never been in a burning building. My life has been remarkably dull, and almost everything I write requires a fair deal of slug labour to find out how things really go. Of my life, all I can reveal is that I play a fair deal of croquet, and since I've never been able to write a book about croquet, everything else has had to be researched."

For his book *Wild One*, Paul Kropp had to go out and take a good look at a horse. "I've always quite despised horses — and I say that straightforwardly — and after I had finished the book, I despised them even more. I think they smell bad and they're quite dangerous and they can hit you with their hooves and do nasty things. I never once, while writing the book, got on a horse.

"So it's possible, I think, through talking to people who have actually lived the experience, to get what I think is a very effective way of presenting it to others. The experience of a flat track bike racer, for instance, who has done it for twenty years, is very different from my experience getting on the thing for the first time."

Paul is continually fiddling with his manuscripts, and he sometimes finds himself taking long showers to organize his thoughts. "I'm very scared, when I let go of the manuscript at the last moment, that there will be something that I should have fixed.

"But the nature of writing a novel is that you keep on working at it until they decide to put it in print."

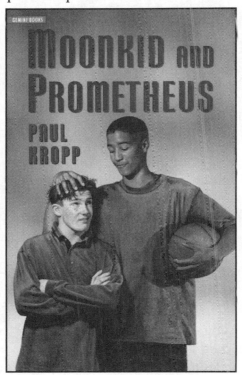

MICHAEL ARVAARLUK KUSUGAK

Born: April 27, 1948,
in Cape Fullerton, Northwest
Territories

Home: Rankin Inlet, Nunavut

SELECTED TITLES

A Promise Is a Promise — 1988

Baseball Bats for Christmas — 1990

Hide and Sneak — 1992

*Northern Lights:
The Soccer Trails* — 1993
(Ruth Schwartz Award)

My Arctic 1, 2, 3 — 1996

Arctic Stories — 1998

Who Wants Rocks? — 1999

"We only spoke Inuktitut when I was little, and there weren't books written in Inuktitut except the Roman Catholic prayer book that we used, so we didn't read a lot," Michael Arvaarluk Kusugak recalls. "What we got more of was storytelling. Storytelling has always been a great tradition with the Inuit. There are legends that have been told from generation to generation for hundreds of years. I grew up in a tiny community called Repulse Bay, where I spent a lot of time at my grandmother's hut. And I think it was from her that I first heard the stories."

After growing up in that close community where stories were told, but rarely read, Michael had to go away to study. "I really didn't read until I started going to school. The very first books that we had were the school readers called *Fun with Dick and Jane*. They were just hideous things, and I don't think anybody ever fell in love with those.

"I went to school in a lot of different places. I had to leave my parents and my community. And I had to go to places away from my people. I went to Yellowknife where there are trees and where — at that time — there were no Inuit. Then I had to go to Churchill, Manitoba, and I graduated from

high school in Saskatoon, Saskatchewan. It was very hard to develop a group of friends. It was so much easier just to sit and write something."

MICHAEL MEETS MUNSCH

In this way, Michael began to develop his skills as a writer, but it wasn't for many years that he finally considered doing it for a living. "I was working for the government of the Northwest Territories, and I had been working for the government for a long time. I had this idea that it was going to be a career until I retired, but I didn't really enjoy it all that much. I joined the library board in Rankin Inlet, and one day when we had a meeting, we invited Robert Munsch. He came and he stayed with us, and I started telling stories. One day, he said, 'Why don't you write them down?' And, as they say, the rest is history."

"History," as Michael calls it, began when he submitted his first story to Annick Press and it was rejected. "It was the most humiliating experience I've ever had, I think. But at the same time, I would imagine that a lot of people get discouraged by that kind of treatment from a publisher, and probably in a lot of cases it's just as well. Because unless you're willing to persevere and keep going after different publishers, I don't think there's any sense in going on."

Now, for all you readers who write and ask Michael, 'How big is an igloo?' here's his answer. "We build three different sizes of igloos. One is for when you go out hunting, and you build an igloo that is just big enough for you and your companion — it's like a pup tent; it's small and easy to build, and it heats up quickly so you don't freeze to death. The second kind is a live-in igloo, which would be big enough for your whole family and it would have a sleeping platform, a bit of a floor and a cooking counter. The third kind is a huge, huge igloo that we build to hold parties in. It's called a *qaggi*."

"Grandmother, please tell me a story."

Michael does not work in an igloo. "I have an office which is right next door to my house. It's a big shed and it's very quiet. Every morning at six-thirty, I get up and I start a pot of coffee. Then I come over here, start up my wood stove and I start to work."

Michael writes his stories in English and not in his native Inuktitut. "I made this decision when I decided to become a writer, because I think you have to write for your audience and the Inuktitut audience is really small — even the Canadian audience is not that big!

"The actual writing part doesn't take all that long. It might take a week or two weeks. Then, after it's done, the real

work starts. The 'real work' is rewriting over and over and over again until it sounds good — until it sounds like somebody has been telling the story for hundreds of years."

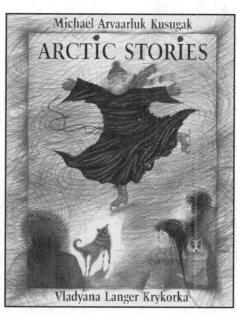

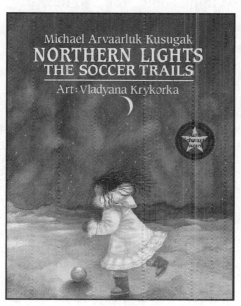

Do It Yourself!

Michael Kusugak remembers an airship flying over Repulse Bay when he was a boy. At the time, his whole community was very afraid because they had never seen anything like it. Michael suggests that you try writing about a historical event from the perspective of someone who witnessed it happening.

KIM LaFAVE

Born: January 12, 1955,
in Vancouver, British Columbia

Home: Roberts Creek,
British Columbia

SELECTED TITLES

The Mare's Egg — 1980

Amos's Sweater — 1988
(Amelia Frances Howard-Gibbom Award,
Governor General's Award)

Canadian Fire Fighters — 1991

Follow that Star — 1994

Bats about Baseball — 1995

I Am Small — 1994

Catalogue — 1998

*Andrew's Magnificent
Mountain of Mittens* — 1998

We'll All Go Sailing — 2001

"I'm the youngest in the family, and when everyone would head off to school, I'd just break out pencils and paper and start drawing," Kim LaFave remembers. "That was my company and my entertainment."

Kim studied commercial art and went on to do illustrations for magazines. But when he was introduced to children's publishing, he found things in the work that he hadn't before. "You had a chance to get a lot more deeply involved in something. The other jobs came in and out pretty quickly, but these ones you had a long time to think about. You had the opportunity to work with interesting people and then, when the book was done, it sort of took on a life of its own."

Now, as it is with most children's book illustrators, Kim receives manuscripts from his publisher and has the opportunity to decide which he'd like to work on. How does he know which to choose? "You receive a lot of manuscripts and if they don't excite you, then you just don't take them on. But every once in a while, one comes along and you just feel very close to the character. I think that's because when I draw, I draw from my imagination and I draw from my experience."

THE YOUNGEST IN THE FAMILY

Such a book was Kim's project with poet Sheree Fitch, entitled *I Am Small*. "It's easy to illustrate a book like that because I was the youngest in the family and I remember being small very, very clearly. I remember everybody's shoes being so much bigger than mine — all those kinds of things that she talks about in the story."

Kim gets up in the morning and starts working almost immediately, because he solves a lot of his illustration problems when he's asleep. He treats each book as if it were one great big illustration.

> *"It was interesting, and I got to work with some great people."*

"I start out with little tiny sketches and scribble them all up really quick, so the first time I do the sketches for a story I may only spend an hour on it." Kim then does detailed final drawings in pencil. "I'm always going back and forth as I go along. It's the same with the finished art, because in the months and months it can take to do the paintings for a book, a lot can happen: the light changes; I start running out of paint so I start using different colours. I want the things that need to be consistent, to be consistent — like the colours, costumes and skin tones — so I'll go through and do all the backgrounds at once, then all the foregrounds, then all the characters. Just so that those things remain consistent."

For Kim, this back-and-forth technique has another advantage. "It gives you that chance for ideas to develop. If you start one and take it right to the finish, then you're kind of committed and you have to do all the rest the same way. Then you know what it's going to turn out like, and then it becomes boring because you know you've got about twenty illustrations you have to make look just like the first one."

Kim notes: "When kids are really young, they're just naturals — they draw and they're totally accepting of everything they do. Then, as they get older, they start to want to draw more perfectly, and they become much more self-conscious and self-aware. The big thing I've found working myself is to keep an open mind, because all those things you start calling mistakes, sometimes are the the best parts of a painting."

Do It Yourself!

Kim LaFave suggests that you make your "mistakes" work for you. The next time you're painting a picture and something doesn't go quite right, don't panic. Take a moment to really look at what you've done before throwing everything away. It may be that a slip of the brush is the best thing that ever happened to your painting!

JULIE LAWSON

Born: November 9, 1947,
in Victoria, British Columbia

Home: Sooke, British Columbia

SELECTED TITLES

*A Morning to Polish
and Keep* — 1992

Kate's Castle — 1992

The Dragon's Pearl — 1992

White Jade Tiger — 1993

*Whatever You Do, Don't
Go Near That Canoe!* — 1996

Emma and the Silk Train — 1997

Goldstone — 1997

Bear on the Train — 1999

Destination Gold! — 2000

*Across the James
Bay Bridge* — 2001

Julie Lawson was a teacher for eighteen years before she decided to pursue writing. "I always thought it would be really neat to write a story that would be made into a book and end up in a library, because I loved going to the library. But getting published was sort of a dream I had at the back of my mind. I never really followed up on it until I turned forty and thought, Time's running out — I'd better do something about it.

"I think I always had a yearning to be a writer. I loved making up stories when I was a kid and writing them down . . . There was one story called 'The One-Eyed Cow' which was very off-the-wall. It actually was my first publication. It was included in an anthology that my grade-eight English teacher put together for us at the end of the year."

Although many of Julie's books have a West Coast connection, she doesn't set out to write only about where she lives. Julie explains, "It's more about getting an idea and thinking, That would be a great story. A lot of things that I remember doing as a child have ended up in my books, so they're West Coast in flavour, too, because I grew up on Vancouver Island."

Julie's book *Destination Gold!* is set in Dawson City in the Yukon Territory. To get a first-hand feel for the city and its history, she applied to the Yukon Arts Council for a five-month winter stay at the Berton House Writers' Retreat in Dawson City. Staying in Pierre Berton's childhood home would place her two minutes from the Dawson City Museum and the Historical Society archives.

> *"I don't come from a writing background, but I certainly do come from a family of readers and great storytellers. I always had a lot of encouragement from my parents to read a lot and to use the library. They always loved to listen to me read my stories, or they read them themselves."*

"That was a fabulous experience, just living up in the North. To experience that real cold was so foreign to me, and a real revelation and very exhilarating. I loved it. I did a lot of writing and soaked up the atmosphere and the northern lights. I could talk about this forever."

A fan of hunting in archives, Julie finds that studying period photographs and newspapers helps her to create an authentic

EMMA AND THE SILK TRAIN

Julie Lawson   Paul Mombourquette

JULIE LAWSON

GOLDSTONE

setting for her stories. But research can be addictive. "The trouble with research is you never know when to stop. If you get bogged down with whatever is happening in your story, you think, Well, I won't waste the whole day. I'll go and do some more research. And then, of course, you want to use it all, which can be a problem, too.

"I'm a very unorganized writer. I don't start with outlines or think about chapters at all, because before I actually get started writing, I never know all the things that are going to happen in the book. So it's just an off-by-the-seat-of-my-pants kind of thing. I always know the time period and a core incident that I want to include. And the more I work on the story, the more the characters become real and they start taking on a life of their own, and they start doing things that had never occurred to me. How that happens I can't explain."

Julie may have come to writing later in life than many, but her career proves that it's possible to begin anew doing something you love and continue to grow with it.

She recalls the question of a curious grade-two student. "She asked me, 'What are you going to be when you grow up?'"

And what was Julie's reply? "I told her I was going to be a writer."

DO IT YOURSELF!

If you have trouble thinking of a story idea, Julie Lawson suggests you try playing the "what if" game. Take something ordinary, like your pen or backpack, and ask yourself, What if this object had magical powers? What would they be? What problems might they cause? Explore the possibilities!

DENNIS LEE

Born: August 31, 1939,
in Toronto, Ontario

Home: Toronto, Ontario

SELECTED TITLES

Wiggle to the Laundromat — 1970

Alligator Pie — 1974
(CLA Book of the Year for Children)

*Nicholas Knock and
Other People* — 1974

Garbage Delight — 1977
(CLA Book of the Year for Children,
Ruth Schwartz Award)

The Ordinary Bath — 1979

Jelly Belly — 1983

Lizzy's Lion — 1984

The Ice Cream Store — 1991
(Mr. Christie's Book Award)

Ping and Pong — 1983

Bubblegum Delicious — 2000

Vicky Metcalf Award winner, 1986

The first time Dennis Lee ever saw his work in print was in a children's magazine called *Wee Wisdom* when he was only nine years old. "I sent in a poem called 'If' which appeared there, and I was so staggered by the Nobel-Prize-winning feel of my achievement that I didn't publish another poem for thirteen years," says Dennis with a laugh.

Dennis Lee is now an experienced poet for children and for adults. He explains that he came up with the idea for what is probably his best-known poem, "Alligator Pie," in a rather unusual way. He had been writing Mother Goose-type rhymes for his own kids, and was on his way to do an errand when it came to him.

"I got on my bike and I had a shopping bag or something slung over my shoulder. I headed off, and as my feet were going round on the pedals, the words started coming into my brain: 'Alligator pie, alligator pie . . . ' to the rhythm of my feet going round. It seemed so airhead that I tried to dismiss it, but it kept coming: 'Alligator pie, alligator pie. If I don't get some I think I'm gonna die.' Finally the thing was bugging me so much, I stopped the bike, turned it around, went back to the house, got a piece of paper and scribbled down however much had come, thinking that that would exorcise it and it wouldn't bother me any more." But, of course, that was just the beginning for Dennis and for "Alligator Pie." Dennis jokes, "It actually became a complete alligator around my neck!"

The collection of poems that eventually became the manuscript for *Alligator Pie* took Dennis over nine years to complete. Dennis met with the publisher at Macmillan, who had some very special testing in mind. Dennis says, "He went out into his neighbourhood, rounded up a batch of kids and said, 'Come on, we're going to sit down and read some poems.' He dragged them into his living room, and he sat and read to them from the manuscript. Of course, there were no pictures or anything like that to hold their interest, but he was satisfied that they were enjoying it, so he got back to me and said, 'We're very interested.' "

ONE BOOK BECOMES TWO

As it turned out, nine years of work had actually produced enough material for two books. Dennis and his publisher decided to split the material in half, creating a book for young children, which would be *Alligator Pie*, and another for older readers, called *Nicholas Knock and Other People*.

Dennis had intended to title his book "Dance Across the Earth," after one of the poems in his collection. But this changed when his publisher joined him at some of his school readings.

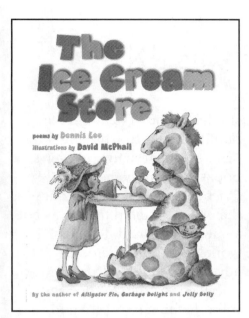

Dennis explains, "He noticed at the end of every one that the kids would come out chanting 'Alligator Pie' to each other, which was just one of thirty or forty poems I might do with them while I was in there, and eventually he said, 'You know, I think you'd better just accept the inevitable. The kids are naming your book for themselves.'" And so it was that *Alligator Pie* found a name.

"I live in Toronto and down on Spadina Avenue there's a twenty-four-hour place that you can call up and say, I'd like one idea, fourteen inches. I need double peppers, double cheese and pepperoni on it."

Although it no longer takes Dennis nine years to write a book, he frequently does as many as fifty drafts of a poem. He likens his writing style to that of many sculptors who sense that the form they hope to carve is already in the stone, believing all that must be done is to chip away everything that isn't the sculpture. "I get that sense with writing. Of course, I have to *generate* the stone in terms of endless drafts in the process, but then I give things permission not to be in the poem, so that the actual poem itself can stand out."

When kids ask Dennis where he gets his ideas, he jokes about ordering them like pizzas, then more seriously explains that, for him, writing depends a great deal on intuition. "Even young children know about intuition — know about discovering things that they know without knowing why they know them."

He then goes on to ask them: How does your body know how to move when you play a sport? How do you know what you want to include next when you're doing a drawing? In a way, it just happens.

DO IT YOURSELF!

Dennis Lee enjoys writing poems that rhyme and free verse poems, too. Write a poem that rhymes, then take the same basic idea and write a poem in free verse.

MICHÈLE LEMIEUX

Born: May 29, 1955,
in Quebec City, Quebec

Home: Montreal, Quebec

SELECTED TITLES

What's that Noise? — 1984

Lucky Hans — 1985

🎨 *Winter Magic* — 1985

🎨 *Amahl and the Night
Visitors* — 1986

🎨 *A Gift from
Saint Francis* — 1989

🎨 *Voices on the Wind:
Poems for all Seasons* — 1990

Peter and the Wolf — 1991

The Pied Piper of Hamelin — 1993

🎨 *The Was an Old Man* — 1994

Stormy Night — 1999
(Elizabeth Mrazik-Cleaver Award)

🎨 — illustrations only

Michèle Lemieux became enchanted with the arts at a very early age. "I spent most of my free time as a child doing crafts and art. I did a lot of puppets; I wrote fairy tales and puppet shows. I had a very good friend who liked doing things like that, and together we did lots of things involving music, writing and drawing.

"Once in school we had an oral assignment where we had to say in front of the class what we would like to do when we grew up. I took this question very seriously, and I remember I felt so terrible because I said I wanted to write books and make pictures inside of them. Everyone else said they wanted to be nurses or teachers or mothers, and I thought, Oh no, I'm all wrong!"

Years later, when she began working as an illustrator, Michèle still felt alone in her desire to publish books for children. "There weren't many children's books being done here in Quebec, and I had the feeling that what I wanted to do was not something I could do here. I worked as an illustrator for advertising and I hated it. So I decided to go to Europe and try something else. I went to Germany for what I thought would be a couple of months, and I stayed for five years. That's where I had my real start." Even now that she's back in Canada, Michèle still tries to get to the European book fairs every year to keep herself motivated.

Inspiration is easy to find for Michèle. "Ideas are everywhere; you just have to notice them. Sit in a bus on a boring day and look at the people. You'll get plenty of ideas. A woman's nose

may be amazing, or the feet of a man sitting next to you may be huge. Very often, I sit on the bus and I try to guess who will come in next. They're all different and they all have different faces, and this is a source of inspiration for me. Just look at what is going on around you. Take it and put it in another context — then it becomes magic."

A Tricky Question

When kids ask Michèle how long it takes to do each picture, she explains that this is a tricky question to answer. "I like to change the medium when I work, and it certainly makes a big difference in the time I spend on a picture. Also, some pictures seem very simple, but I may have to redo them five or six times before I'm happy with them. Say the last picture I do is the one I pick, and it took me three hours. But it's the fifth time I did it, so it actually took me a week."

"I spend a lot of time questioning myself."

"When I work, if I'm too stiff or I'm not concentrating or I'm just not achieving what I want, very often I just stop and paint anything that comes into my head. Then I go back to the picture, and it goes much better." This technique, Michèle admits, may also extend the time it takes to complete an illustration.

When she has time off from her work as an illustrator and a teacher at Université du Québec à Montréal, Michèle enjoys visiting

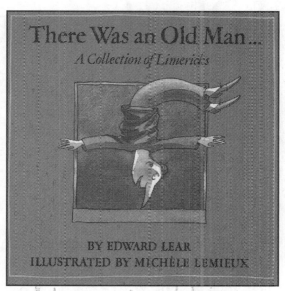

There Was an Old Man...
A Collection of Limericks

BY EDWARD LEAR
ILLUSTRATED BY MICHÈLE LEMIEUX

kids in schools. Often, at the end of her visit, she'll do an original drawing for the class. On a huge piece of paper, she'll draw a simple character, then she'll ask the class questions about her picture, drawing what the kids ask her to draw. For instance, a picture which begins as a plain little pig could end up being a granny pig going to the park with her grandson, or it could be a punk pig on his way to rob a bank. It always turns out differently. And it always gives her a good idea about what kids like.

Back when she was first starting out and feeling discouraged, Michèle remembered how much she loved what she was doing and resolved to continue, saying, "I want to keep going until someone can prove to me that what I do is bad and ugly and stupid and children hate it." Needless to say, this has never happened. And we're all very glad about that.

Do It Yourself!

Michèle Lemieux suggests you make one list of objects and a second of animals. Then choose one thing from each list and combine drawings of both to create one creature. Can you imagine, for example, what a hat and a rabbit would look like if they were drawn as one creature? What about a horse and a bench?

RON LIGHTBURN

Born: June 24, 1954,
in Cobourg, Ontario

Home: Kentville, Nova Scotia

SELECTED TITLES

Waiting for the Whales — 1991
(Amelia Frances Howard-Gibbon Award,
Elizabeth Mrazik-Cleaver Award,
Governor General's Award)

I Can't Sleep — 1992

Eagle Dreams — 1994

How Smudge Came — 1995
(Mr. Christie's Book Award)

Driftwood Cove — 1998

Wild Girl and Gran — 2000

Ron Lightburn was born in Cobourg, Ontario, and moved with his family to Vancouver, British Columbia, when he was four. The child of British immigrants, his first books were the *Rupert* annuals from England.

Ron recalls, "I was able to follow the stories before I learned how to read, because they were told so well visually. The man who wrote and drew those *Rupert* annuals when I was young was a wonderful artist named Alfred Bestall. I still have all of my old *Ruperts*, and I can see their influence on my artwork."

It wasn't long before Ron decided to make some books of his own. He explains, "My tales of dinosaurs and robots were so popular that other kids wanted to own them (and teachers wanted to confiscate them). Comic books

Wild Girl & Gran
NAN GREGORY • PAINTINGS BY RON LIGHTBURN

at the store cost twelve cents, so I priced mine at five cents. To my surprise, they sold. So I had my first inkling, at age eight, that there might be a career in storytelling and artwork."

> *"In junior high, I was reading science-fiction novels and collected the pocket books as much for their cover art as for the stories."*

Ron has used pencil crayons to draw everything from those early comic books to award-winning children's book illustrations, although he recently began using oil paints exclusively. "This isn't surprising, as the work of many of the illustrators I've admired and studied over the years was rendered with oils. I find that oil paintings have a depth and richness that's difficult to duplicate with other media.

"I use a realistic style of artwork for many of my projects, and this often requires me to research my subject matter so that all of the details are accurate. This may only involve a trip to the library, though sometimes I have to dig deeper. For *Eagle Dreams*, a story about a boy who finds an injured eagle near his family's dairy farm, I spent a couple of days with real vets as they made their rounds of local farms."

Ron likes the people he paints to look natural, so he generally uses models for the characters in the stories. "Often I'll ask friends or neighbours if they'd like to pose for me. When I look at my illustrations from *Waiting for the Whales* and *Driftwood Cove*, it's like seeing a photo album of my friends in Victoria, BC."

When he's given a story to illustrate, Ron always tries to ensure that the words and the pictures he creates are in perfect harmony. "I also try to contribute my own ideas that will help to tell the story. For example, in *Waiting for the Whales*, I gave the old man in the story a hat, because it seemed natural to me that someone who spends a great deal of time outside would wear a hat. And even though his hat is not mentioned in the text, it becomes an important symbol for the knowledge and responsibility that is passed on to his granddaughter."

A BRIGHT PLACE TO WORK

"I work at home and use the living room of our house as my studio because it has the largest windows. I prefer to work by natural light whenever possible. I'm usually at my easel by eight-thirty AM, and try to wrap things up by three or four o'clock in the afternoon. I don't like to work in the evenings or on weekends, but sometimes find it necessary in order to meet a deadline. I don't use the computer too much, mainly because I don't like staring at a screen for long periods of time. When I want a break from painting, I'll sit back

with a cup of tea and mull over what I've accomplished. Or I'll have an apple and go for a walk outside, which gives me a fresh perspective on things when I return to the easel."

When he visits schools, Ron is often asked about the ins and outs of pursuing a career as an illustrator. He remembers one student who got right to the point. "He said, 'Let's talk cash flow.' He had a good point. After all, when you're in business for yourself, you have to be able to budget your finances properly. If you don't do it, then who will? So I always suggest that, in conjunction with studying writing and/or artwork, every future author and illustrator should learn something about investments and financial management. The life of a freelancer is anything but stable, so it is especially important for those of us in the literary world to manage our precious royalties very carefully. So start those RRSPs early and marvel at the miracle of compound interest!"

DO IT YOURSELF!

When Ron Lightburn did the illustrations for his book *I Can't Sleep*, he used dark blue paper as the background for his night scenes to create a dramatic mood. The next time you draw a picture, why not begin with a sheet of orange paper to represent a dusky sky or green paper for a grassy field?

JEAN LITTLE

Born: January 2, 1932,
in Taipei, Taiwan

Home: Guelph, Ontario

SELECTED TITLES

Mine for Keeps — 1962

Listen for the Singing — 1977
(Canada Council Prize)

*Mama's Going to Buy You
a Mockingbird* — 1984
(CLA Book of the Year for Children,
Ruth Schwartz Award)

Hey, World, Here I Am! — 1986

Jess Was the Brave One — 1991

His Banner Over Me — 1996

The Belonging Place — 1997

Willow and Twig — 2000
(Mr. Christie's Book Award)

Emma's Yucky Brother — 2001

Orphan at My Door — 2001

Vicky Metcalf Award winner, 1974

"All my family inspired me to be interested in books," Jean Little recalls. "Then out of the interest in books came the interest in writing."

And so Jean chose her profession accordingly. "I always wanted to write, but I was going to teach to make a living — people had told me for years you couldn't make a living as a writer." But that hasn't turned out to be true for Jean. In fact, not long after she published her first books, she gave up teaching full time to take up a career in writing — although she still works with kids and writers in classroom settings.

Jean describes her first publishing experience as marvellous. "I finished the book to the best of my ability — I had a lot of fun writing it — and sent it in to a competition and won. Right away I got a thousand-dollar publisher's prize which was an advance on royalties, and the story was published. I remember the editor coming up from Boston to take me out to lunch, and that was extremely exciting."

CREATING REAL CHARACTERS

When kids ask Jean if her characters are based on real people, Jean replies, "They're usually more real to me than the children who ask the question are, because they have a long life that no living child will have. Anna [in her book *From Anna*]

will always be nine, even though in another book she's fourteen. Because you can always open up the book and she's nine again, and she'll do that forever, as long as there is a book."

Jean goes on to say, "My characters are real enough that if I get halfway through writing a book and decide I don't want to finish it, what makes me finish it is the characters. Because if I don't finish it, it's like killing them. Their only chance to live is if I finish the book."

Another reason Jean Little's characters are so real to her is that they're largely based on her memories. Just read her autobiographical books, *Little by Little* and *Stars Come Out Within*, and you'll see that many characters and events from her own childhood have crept into her stories.

Jean says that she wrote these books about her childhood

74

because she was always having to complete the biographical questionnaires her publishers sent her. "I hate filling out forms. My life sounds so devoid of interest. It seems like all I've done is go to school and write books. It seems so deadly dull, and yet it isn't really like that at all."

"My family were all readers. We read aloud and read together and read separately."

Does Jean write from an outline? "Never! In my head I sort of know what's coming, but one of the things that keeps me writing — and this is for sure — is the delight of discovering stuff. I like not knowing what's going to happen at any given moment. It's like working on a puzzle, except that you're far more emotionally involved."

When Jean can't find information to describe something in her books, she finds a way of getting around it. "Years ago, Lorrie McLaughlin told me that there was a sea battle in one of her books and she didn't know what the ships looked like, so she put the kid up a tree where he could hear the battle — because she knew how it would sound — but where he couldn't see anything because of the leaves. If the research isn't pertinent to the plot, you don't need to do it. You can avoid it."

And what is Jean's advice for kids who want to become writers? "Write on Saturdays.

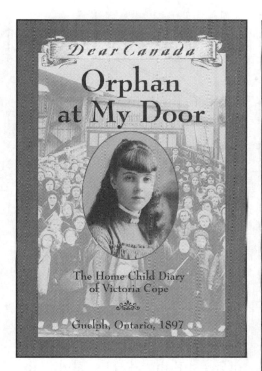

Dear Canada
Orphan at My Door

The Home Child Diary of Victoria Cope

Guelph, Ontario, 1897

Don't just write when a teacher says, Now it's time for writing. If you want to write, you have to be able to motivate yourself. Starting is half the battle. One way to do that is to write on holidays, write on Saturdays and write on your own time, so you can learn how to make yourself get going and do it."

JANET LUNN

Born: December 28, 1928,
in Dallas, Texas, USA

Home: Ottawa, Ontario

SELECTED TITLES

*The Twelve Dancing
Princesses* — 1979
(Canada Council Prize)

The Root Cellar — 1981
(CLA Book of the Year for Children)

Amos's Sweater — 1988
(Ruth Schwartz Award)

Shadow in Hawthorn Bay — 1988
(Canada Council Prize,
CLA Book of the Year for Children,
CLA Young Adult Book Award)

Duck Cakes for Sale — 1989

*One Hundred Shining
Candles* — 1990

The Story of Canada — 1995
(Information Book Award,
Mr. Christie's Book Award)

Come to the Fair — 1997

The Hollow Tree — 1997
(Governor General's Award)

The Umbrella Party — 1998

Vicky Metcalf Award winner, 1982

Janet Lunn's first job was in a local public library in Rye, New York, where she grew up and where she's sure that even today she'd be able to find the collection of E. Nesbit books she so loved as a child. Her all-time favourite, however, was *The Secret Garden* by Frances Hodgson Burnett. "I read it still about once a year!"

Part of the reason young readers today are as entranced by Janet's books as she was by those of her childhood is her ability to transport her readers to another place and time. "As a writer of historical fiction, a lot of time is spent researching. I don't want to write about a place that my feet haven't been. If I'm going to take you to the north of Scotland, I've got to have been there so I know what it feels like. And then, of course, there's reading the history of the time, reading about the music, the costume. There's a lot of stuff to look up, but I always travel to the places that I'm writing about."

Janet doesn't decide to write stories about places she'd like to visit, though; in fact, she never knows where she's going to have to go until the idea for a story comes to her. And that idea can come from absolutely anywhere. "*The Root Cellar* is about my own house where I do have a ghost, and *Amos's Sweater* is very definitely about a sheep that I met.

"I have ideas backed up like people trying to get into a fast-food restaurant. Those are the ones I think I'll write next, but then some other idea marches right up to the front of the line and pushes everybody else out."

When Janet has decided on one idea, she isn't always eager to begin. "The part that frightens me is actually plunging into a new book. I'm so scared of it. I know that when I start writing, I'm going to be lost in that world for two, three, four years, and so I shy away from it."

> *"I probably made the
> decision to become
> a writer around the
> time I decided to
> have feet."*

But when Janet does get going, there's almost no stopping her. Even when she's finished, she can't help making endless adjustments. "I like rewriting — obviously, or I wouldn't do it so much. Some people just hate it, but not me." Janet's love of editing is so great that she admits she could easily be rewriting forever, and recalls a favourite story about a famous French painter who, when he was a very old man, would go to the Louvre and touch up his paintings while his friends kept the guards busy. Janet allows that it's harder to fiddle with a book once it's printed, but she does make small changes when she reads her work out loud to students.

In fact, reading aloud is a big part of Janet's revision process. "When you read something out loud to yourself, you don't hear the flaws the way you do when you read it to an audience. It doesn't require that a person tell you all the things they think are right and wrong; it's just that your antennae are much more out there when you've got someone listening to you."

For Janet Lunn, the only thing as hard as starting a book is finishing it. "I mourn a book that's finished — not the history, but the fiction that I really get involved in. I mourn that, when it's over. You live with these people a long time, and closely. I still remember the day I called the publisher to see if the book *The Root Cellar* was ready. She said, 'Yup, they're here, you can

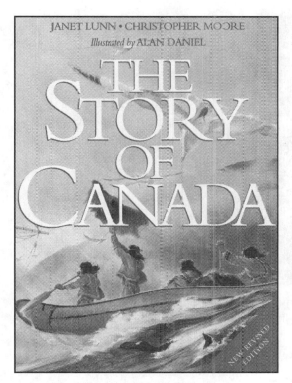

come and get yours,' and I sat down and cried because I knew it really was over."

Janet says this mourning is similar to the feeling you get when you come to the end of a great book and realize that you have to let those characters go "except that instead of having had one reading experience, you've lived with these people for a couple of years. And suddenly it's over. You realize you can go and visit, but it's not the same.

"Then, of course, I'm fickle, and the next thing I know I'm into a new one."

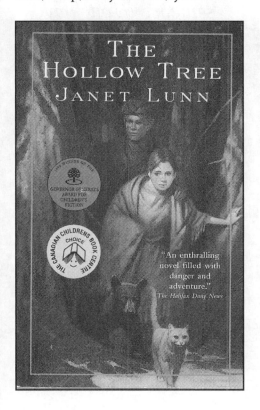

DO IT YOURSELF!

Janet Lunn believes that in order to train yourself as a writer, you have to use your eyes like a painter does: you need to look at things and be able to describe them. If you're really serious about writing, every day describe something new. Use the best few words you can find in your description.

CLAIRE MACKAY

Born: December 21, 1930, in Toronto, Ontario

Home: Toronto, Ontario

SELECTED TITLES

Mini-Bike Hero — 1974

Exit Barney McGee — 1979

One Proud Summer — 1981
(Ruth Schwartz Award)

Mini-Bike Rescue — 1982

Pay Cheques and Picket Lines: All About Unions in Canada — 1987

The Toronto Story — 1990

Touching All the Bases — 1994

Bats About Baseball — 1994

Laughs (editor) — 1997

First Folks and Vile Voyageurs — 2001

Vicky Metcalf Award winner, 1983

"I always had it in the back of my mind from a very early age that I would write; although I'm not sure that I said to myself, I think I will be an author," Claire Mackay says. "I loved words and I loved putting them together. I even did it when I didn't have to. I think that's probably a tip-off — that you eventually make your way to your proper vocation."

Claire remembers the encouraging words of a teacher. "In high school, I had an absolutely marvellous English teacher in grades twelve and thirteen. He actually suggested that I could be a journalist, and I just about fell down and licked his shoes at that point. I did try in college. I went and applied at the college paper, but my first story for *The Varsity* just didn't cut it — that was my first and last story. It was so full of flowery description that they felt my talents didn't quite match their needs."

Despite this first job — or perhaps because of it — Claire put off a serious attempt at writing for a long time. This, she says, was partly because there were no role models around — at least not like there are today, as Claire and other notable writers visit classrooms across the country.

IN SEARCH OF A ROLE MODEL

"Nobody came to our school and said, I write books. So I had this vision — which was highly romanticized, I'm sure — of some distant person in an English castle writing books. That was one of the reasons that I neglected to apply myself to what I should have been doing all my life. The other reason was that I was very fearful. I had read so much good stuff that I had somehow achieved the notion that I could never be very good — that if I couldn't be excellent, then why try — which is a really self-defeating way to go about your life. Nevertheless, I was afraid that I would just make a hash of it, so I delayed trying it until close to middle age."

> *"If I can write a fine sentence in one day, I can be happy the whole day."*

Claire rediscovered her desire to write when, as an adult student, another teacher suggested she give creative writing a try. She found she was better suited to writing fiction than she was to newspaper work, and when her first book, *Mini-Bike Hero*, was submitted to a publisher, it was accepted at once. "No one was more astonished than I, and I haven't had any problems since. It just turned my life completely around."

In fact, the biggest surprise for Claire was the fact that everyone began calling her a writer. "I had some notion that nobody would notice that this book had been written, and that I had written it — although I don't how I thought I could be anonymous because the first printing sold out in about four months. All of a sudden people were calling me a writer; I personally could not apply that noun to myself for the first four books. I used to whisper it. People would ask me what I do, and I'd say, 'Oh, I'm a writer.'"

Claire is embarrassed to admit that she works better if someone is hanging over her saying, Get that done. And she confesses to being a terrible procrastinator. She reads mystery stories and makes lists to waste time, but she has one truly unusual habit, too. "I think about a word that I want to use, and I look it up in the dictionary. Then I begin to read the dictionary!" Claire says she can amuse herself for hours this way, since she collects dictionaries and owns well over a hundred of them.

Claire Mackay has another important place in the Canadian writers' community. She is one of the eleven founding members of the Canadian Society of Children's Authors, Illustrators and Performers (CANSCAIP), an organization devoted to encouraging those interested in working in these fields. Since it was founded, professional membership has swelled to over four hundred members and associate membership is well over a thousand. Claire says, "I've been astonished by its growth, but I think the growth

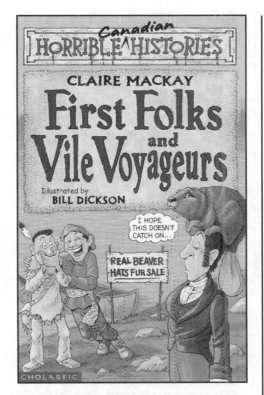

validated the original impulse. Yes, we do need something for creators of young people's materials."

DO IT YOURSELF!

Claire Mackay believes strongly that writing poetry and verse is the best training for all writers. You must be aware of the rhythm, root and weight of the words you're using, and you must be able to use them effectively in a very structured way. She suggests that you try writing a sonnet, ballad, quatrain or rondo. Before you begin, ask your teacher to help you determine how each of these kinds of poems is constructed.

KEVIN MAJOR

Born: September 12, 1949,
in Stephenville, Newfoundland

Home: St. John's, Newfoundland

SELECTED TITLES

Hold Fast — 1978
(Canada Council Prize, CLA Book of the Year
for Children, Ruth Schwartz Award)

Far from Shore — 1980
(CLA Young Adult Book Award)

Thirty-Six Exposures — 1984

Dear Bruce Springsteen — 1987

Blood Red Ochre — 1989

Eating Between the Lines — 1991

Diana: My Autobiography — 1993
(CLA Book of the Year for Children)

*The House of
Wooden Santas* — 1997
(Mr. Christie's Book Award)

Free the Children — 1998

*Eh? to Zed: A Canadian
ABeCedarium* — 2000

A hockey player and a Frank Mahovlich fan, Kevin Major did not do much reading when he was young. And he didn't seriously begin to write until he was teaching at a junior high school in the 1970s. "There weren't many books around that had characters in them much like the characters that were in my classroom — no really contemporary Newfoundland novels, and very few Canadian ones."

Kevin says that it was this realization, combined with his own memories of the confusing and worrisome experiences of being a teenager, which made him decide to write for young people. Kevin describes the acceptance of his novel *Hold Fast* as a great relief — after having tried without success to have an earlier work published.

MOVING ON

What made Kevin finally decide to discard that first effort and move on? "It was a combination of things. One, I kept getting all these rejections. A number of them did say, We think you have potential as a writer, but we don't think this particular book is worth publishing. And I can remember one letter saying, You live in a very interesting place in the world; can't you write about real people and real situations? I really hadn't done that with the first effort, and I suppose all

these things were enough encouragement to think that I could put it aside and start fresh. I was really glad that I did, and I'm very glad now that that book wasn't published."

Although Kevin did take the publisher's advice and begin writing about real people and real situations, he has never written about himself in his novels. "I have to say there's a little bit of me in each of them, I guess; a writer can't help but bring some of himself to the book. But I've never taken my own growing-up period and developed a story from that time, with myself disguised as the central character. There are some characters who in personality and temperament have a lot of me in them, but I've tended to take them out of my own particular time period and put them in a more recent era."

Kevin prefers to work without any distractions, and even wears ear plugs if other people are in the house making noise. He tries to get in five solid hours of writing a day and rarely runs out of ideas.

However, he says, "If things are sort of stalled, what I will do is just take time away and read the whole thing through — what I've written so far — and try in some way to outline where this book is going in a total sense, so that I don't just get characters in situations and not know what's going to happen to them next."

When a manuscript is finished, Kevin sends it off to his editor and waits for his or her suggestions. "Sometimes it's quite difficult. I've had disagreements in the past with editors about things that, to me, were very important. And I've had to debate in my mind about how strongly I felt about these particular points and how much ground I could hold, bearing in mind that I

know the editor comes with a fresh perspective on it. A very important part of publishing fiction is to work with the editor."

> *"If I go for periods of time and am unable to write, I get rather cranky."*

Kevin says that his first comic fantasy, *Eating Between the Lines*, was probably the most difficult time he's ever had working with an editor, because the first person who looked at it didn't like the manuscript at all. "That was, I suppose, the most crucial point in any editor/writer relationship. In that case, I came to the point of having to withdraw the book, change editors and move on, because I really had felt that I had done something good with this book and I wanted to see it published."

Once again displaying a terrific knack for knowing what to discard or — perhaps more important in this case — what not to discard, Kevin found another publisher who did like his novel and even won some awards when it was published!

DO IT YOURSELF!

In his book *Eating Between the Lines*, Kevin Major writes about a character who has a magic coin which enables him to go directly into the stories he's reading. Kevin suggests that you use that same coin to go into a favourite book and discover which characters you might become. Then write a story to describe what will happen.

THE HOUSE OF
WOODEN SANTAS

STORY BY KEVIN MAJOR
WOOD CARVINGS BY IMELDA GEORGE

MICHAEL MARTCHENKO

Born: August 1, 1942,
in Carcassonne, France

Home: Toronto, Ontario

SELECTED TITLES

The Paper Bag Princess — 1980

Mortimer — 1983

*Matthew and the
Midnight Tow Truck* — 1984

Thomas's Snowsuit — 1986
(Ruth Schwartz Award)

Pigs — 1989

Wait and See — 1993

Alligator Baby — 1997

High Flight — 1999

*Matthew and the
Midnight Banker* — 2000

Up, Up, Down — 2001

Michael Martchenko describes his young self as a comic-book addict. "I used to go around the neighbourhood trading; that was our thing. Not too many kids had TVs, I guess, so we used to carry a bag of 'traders' under each arm and off we'd go, trading comics."

Michael's favourites were always the ones with really great paintings on the covers, and he recalls being particularly fond of *The Lone Ranger* and *Tarzan*.

"I always knew what I wanted to do. I was always interested in art and drew. I used to fill notebooks drawing little sketches, and I used to copy comic-book characters. For every project in school, if I had the opportunity, I would illustrate."

> *"To me, [that first book] was just another freelance job; I didn't know it was going to change my life."*

It's no surprise to Michael, then, that he found his way into the business of enhancing stories with illustrations himself.

When Michael begins the illustrations for a story, this is what he does: "I read it once, and then I read it twice. Then I suddenly start getting mind pictures, and I do what's called thumbnail sketches. I do them on twelve little squares that I've drawn — only about two inches high — and I just do it quickly; it's almost like if I don't do it fast enough, I'll lose it."

Michael then considers each thumbnail very carefully and makes any changes he feels are necessary. Then he does full-sized pencil sketches.

MORE BOOK FOR YOUR BUCK

Michael jokes about wanting to give his readers more book for their buck by including extra little things in his pictures. "I would say I'm inspired by what I read, but I also like to add a lot of things to the illustrations that are not necessarily covered in the story. Rather than just having a girl and a boy talking on the street, I might do some silly little scene going on behind them — nothing too distracting, but something that kids would get a kick out of."

When he was starting out, Michael's daughter, Holly, and her friend, Helen, used to give him valuable feedback. "I would do my pencil sketches and then I'd say, Okay guys, come here. Sit down and I'm going to read you a story and show you some drawings. And I would read a segment and put up the drawing. They would stare at it and I'd watch their reactions. Then I'd say, What do you think? or What's the matter with it?"

Michael found this input helpful — until Holly grew up. Now, he's more comfortable

judging for himself what works and what doesn't work, so he relies only on the author and his publisher for suggestions.

Although Michael's sketches rarely require major changes, he understands about being flexible. For example, in the preliminary sketches for his first book, *The Paper Bag Princess*, there was a picture of the princess punching Prince Ronald in the nose at the end of the story. But when Robert Munsch and the publisher opted for a less violent ending, Michael changed his sketches to show the princess skipping triumphantly off into the sunset.

In the beginning, Michael worked at an advertising agency during the day and did his books at night and on the weekends. Now a full-time illustrator, he's finding new ways of managing his time. "It took a while to get used to the fact that I could do this stuff during the day. And then I thought, I wonder if I *can* do this stuff during the day; maybe I'm strictly a nocturnal illustrator!"

Whichever hours he works, Michael is extremely dedicated to the quality of his work, and his readers appreciate that. In fact, one young fan actually sent Michael two dollars for doing such a good job! "I put all I can into it because there's nothing worse than having a book published, then looking at it and going, Oh, I wish I hadn't done that. Or, If only I'd done this, and I didn't do it because I was rushing." It's that kind of dedication and discipline which has kept Michael Martchenko happy and very, very busy.

DO IT YOURSELF!

When he was young, Michael Martchenko practised drawing by creating new art for his favourite comics. He suggests you draw new pictures for the text of your favourite story.

CAROL MATAS

Born: November 14, 1949,
in Winnipeg, Manitoba

Home: Winnipeg, Manitoba

SELECTED TITLES

The DNA Dimension — 1982

Lisa — 1987
(Geoffrey Bilson Award)

Sworn Enemies — 1993

Daniel's Story — 1993
(Silver Birch Award)

Of Two Minds — 1995

After the War — 1996
(Red Maple Award)

Greater than Angels — 1998

Cloning Miranda — 1999

In My Enemy's House — 1999

The War Within — 2001

Footsteps in the Snow — 2002

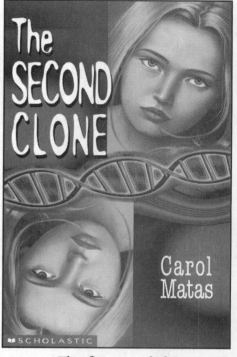

Carol Matas never really gave much thought to a career in writing. "I'd always wanted to be an actor; that was my goal in life. I went away to theatre school and I was acting in Toronto, where I happened to be hanging out with a group of actors who were writing. A number of them were writing plays, but some of them were also writing prose.

"They used to share their stories back and forth, very much like the kids do in schools today. We'd get together in the afternoon or for dinner, and people would read what they'd written. One of these stories was a fantasy about a raindrop, and I was so taken by it. I thought, That really sounds like fun; I think I'll try that. I went home and sat down and wrote my first story, which happened to be a fantasy. I never would have said, I'm going to write children's books. It just so happened that I wrote a fantasy and the protagonists were both children.

"I read it to my friends and they loved it; they thought it was great. So I thought, Well, okay, I'll write another one. I did that for years and the stories kept getting longer. The first one was about five pages; the next was maybe ten; the next one was fifteen."

Carol lost some of this momentum when she got married, and it wasn't until she was pregnant with her first child that she resumed her writing in earnest. The first novel she wrote was another fantasy; the second was *The Fusion Factor*.

"There was a point in there where I almost gave it up because I'd written two; I'd written the fantasy and I'd written *The Fusion Factor* [later retitled *It's Up to Us*] and I'd written a number of short stories and none of them were being published. I thought, Well, maybe it's time to give it up. But at that time somebody from Nelson offered me a contract for one of my short stories. They never did publish it, but I was so encouraged that I said, I won't give it up, and I kept plugging away at *The DNA Dimension*."

The DNA Dimension was accepted right away and *The Fusion Factor* soon found its way into print, too. And Carol decided that maybe she was destined to become a writer, and not an actor, after all.

COMBINING IDEAS

Where does Carol get her ideas? *The DNA Dimension* came about after Carol had watched the movie *Apocalypse Now* and after she had seen a public television series dealing with the difficult choices we're forced to make, as genetic engineering becomes more prevalent. She combined ideas from both to write a story about politicians who believe they're doing the right thing for the people, but aren't.

"Read a lot; that's what I did. It doesn't matter what you read — read everything; read what you like!"

Today Carol takes her inspiration from whatever is interesting her at the moment. "I got interested in *Lisa* and *Jesper* because my husband started telling me stories about what had happened to his family during the war. Then I was given a book about the rescue of the Danish Jews. I didn't know anything about it, so I figured that most Canadian kids probably didn't know the story, either. I thought it was a really important story to tell."

Carol was right to think that young readers would want to know more about this important part of history. Since her stories about the Danish Jews were

published, Carol has received all kinds of encouraging letters from kids, describing how much they've enjoyed her books.

Carol recalls here her own connection with books when she was in school: "I'd eat my lunch, then I'd go up to my room and lie on my bed and read. That was my favourite thing to do at lunch hour. I guess it sort of calmed me down and got me ready for the afternoon. I really liked that quiet time. Even now when I'm touring schools, I wish I could do that. I wish at lunch hour somebody would let me go into a room by myself and lie down and read for half an hour!"

DO IT YOURSELF!

Carol Matas prefers to write about things that interest her. What's interesting you the most right now? Write about that.

NORAH MCCLINTOCK

Born: March 11,
in Pointe Claire, Quebec

Home: Toronto, Ontario

SELECTED TITLES

Shakespeare and Legs — 1987

The Stepfather Game — 1990

Jack's Back — 1992

Mistaken Identity — 1995
(Arthur Ellis Award)

The Body in the Basement — 1997
(Arthur Ellis Award)

Sins of the Father — 1998
(Arthur Ellis Award)

Password: Murder — 1999

Over the Edge — 2000

Scared to Death — 2001

Body, Crime, Suspect — 2001

Norah McClintock exclaims, "Books are my favourite things in the world — well, next to my family!

"When I was a kid, I was lucky enough to live very close to the public library. At the time, a library card cost ten cents. I couldn't think of a better way to spend a dime. That ten cents entitled me to go to the library any time I wanted, stay as long as I wanted, take home whatever books I wanted and keep them for two weeks.

"I still remember one of the oddest and most interesting books I ever found there. It was an old book on secret codes, published sometime just after World War I. The thick little book contained dozens of ways to compose secret messages, using codes that would be difficult to crack. I still have a notebook in my filing cabinet filled with coded messages. The trouble is, I can't remember how to decode them, so they're all a mystery to me now."

Norah says one of the nicest things about being a writer is that you can work anywhere. She jokes, "Sometimes it doesn't look like you're working, though. It looks more like you're daydreaming. A big part of writing is thinking — what would your hero do in a certain situation? What nasty surprise is your villain planning? You have to think about all of these things before you try to put them down on paper. The entire plot of one of my mysteries came to me while I was taking a long, leisurely bubble bath."

Norah's ideas come "from anywhere and everywhere. My very first book, about a tall girl who finds herself romantically pursued by a short boy, comes from my own life. Although I'm not tall enough to play on the NBA, I was usually the only girl in the back row on class picture day. I remember perfectly going to a dance in grade seven. All the boys who asked me to dance were much, much shorter than me, which made me feel very self-conscious. It didn't help that I was — and still am — a very shy person."

LOOMING DEADLINES

Kids and authors have something in common: their assignments must be handed in on time. Norah explains how she deals with a looming deadline: "When I have a piece of work that I need to finish, I work backwards. If the revisions of a novel are due in seven days and the manuscript is 160 pages long, I divide those 160 pages into equal chunks and make sure that I do at least one chunk every day until I reach my deadline."

Having met her deadlines for everything from newspaper articles to brochures, annual reports to mysteries, Norah McClintock has learned a thing or two about being a writer.

"One, rejection isn't the end of the world — although it can sometimes make you doubt yourself and your abilities. But, like anything else, the hurt passes. After a while, once you've realized that you'll survive, it's no big deal.

"Books on shelves, books in stacks on tables, books in boxes in my basement, a tall pile of books on the floor beside my bed — sometimes I think I live in a very messy library!"

"Two, the best part of writing is writing. Yes, it's a thrill to hold in your hands a book that has your name on it. But by the time that happens, it's been a year or more since you wrote the story and you're in the middle of something else which, by then, seems much more interesting and exciting. The book you've written is just a by-product of creativity. Exercising your creativity is where the real excitement comes from.

"And, three, inspiration is just the beginning. It's great, but it won't get you from Chapter One to The End. Writing doesn't just happen. You have to work at it. You have to think and plan and write and then rewrite (and rewrite and rewrite). But, frankly, I can't think of anything else I'd rather do."

DO IT YOURSELF!

If you don't want readers to be able to guess what happens next in your story, try this tip from Norah McClintock. When your character has a problem or needs to get out of a tough situation, don't use the first solution you think of — readers will probably think of that, too. Instead, force yourself to write down five or six different solutions. Then look them over. You'll be surprised by what you've come up with, and so will your readers.

TOLOLWA M. MOLLEL

Born: June 25, 1952,
in Arusha, Tanzania

Home: Edmonton, Alberta

SELECTED TITLES

The Orphan Boy — 1991

The King and the Tortoise — 1993

Rhinos for Lunch and Elephants for Supper! — 1991

Big Boy — 1995

The Flying Tortoise — 1994

Ananse's Feast — 1997

Shadow Dance — 1998

My Rows and Piles of Coins — 1999

Subira, Subira — 2000

To Dinner, For Dinner — 2000

"I grew up in Tanzania and the schools I went to usually had donated books. They got a real mishmash of books — *Treasure Island*, Greek mythology, *The Little Red Hen*. I remember in one school they had American encyclopedias and a friend of mine and I started reading from the beginning because we had run out of material to read. We read about everything."

Tololwa Mollel remembers, "There was no TV and there were no toys. You made your own toys. We were pretty good at doing that. Storytelling was very big. It was a way of life because of the oral nature of the culture and because visiting was very important. The art of talking was really highly regarded. It was called 'eating words.' You had to be able to weave language skilfully. I guess all of that kind of trains one to be a storyteller."

Tololwa's storytelling ability would eventually draw him toward theatre. "I think it was my interest in books and writing that got me into theatre. I was in high school, and out of the blue I said, 'Why don't we do a play?'

"And so I joined theatre. There was quite a bit of writing in theatre because there were only three of us in our class — theatre was not very popular. There weren't that many plays suitable for a Tanzanian audience that had three characters, so we had to create our own plays."

For years, Tololwa also wrote

stories without ever considering sending them to a publisher. And then he learned that *Cricket* magazine's office was located in the same American town where his brother lived. While on a visit to Canada, Tololwa paid *Cricket* a visit. He was encouraged to send in his work, and when he returned home, he submitted ten of his stories all the way from Tanzania. In 1987 Tololwa's first story was accepted.

"I used to not want to talk about an idea that I was working on, because I felt that I would talk the story away, then I wouldn't do it — but not anymore. Now when I talk about an idea, it's a way of making it concrete for myself, a way of thinking about it some more."

He would eventually return to Canada to pursue a master's degree at the University of Alberta, and Edmonton would become his permanent home.

But Tololwa gets much of his inspiration from his birthplace. Many of his stories are based on African folk tales, which he enriches and makes his own with details from similar folk tales from other cultures and from his own life. And songs from his childhood sometimes show up in Tololwa's work, too. "Some of them are pretty catchy and you just want to sing them again and again."

Several years and books later, Tololwa loves what he does, but he still wouldn't call it easy. "I don't find writing easy, but I don't really mind the hard work involved in it. I find the pay-off to be much better than it is in theatre — maybe because I call the shots. I find the hard work to be enjoyable because I know if I run into any problems, I can always count on myself to get me through."

Don't Hurry

Tololwa says, "In the heat of the moment, when I'm writing a story, sometimes I think it's the best thing ever put on paper, and my first inclination is to finish it and rush it off to a publisher. Then I find that I've rushed it, and it comes back with all these comments. Then I'm kind of angry with the whole publishing world. I think, Who do they think they are? Don't they know how hard it is to write a story? But that only lasts for about a day or two, and then I look at the story and say, Yeah, maybe they're right; I felt it in my bones, but I kind of suppressed it. Then I'll put it away, or sometimes I can find a way of making it better."

Tololwa offers young writers some advice that he says he has trouble following himself. "Have patience. Stories have a life of their own. They grow at their own pace. You can't really hurry them along. The story will tell you when it's ready. I think one has to have the patience to hold back for better and better ideas and better words. I find patience to be the hardest thing to attain. I have a story. I want it ready. I want to share it and I want everybody to see how good it is. I have to remind myself to learn to hold it back as long as possible."

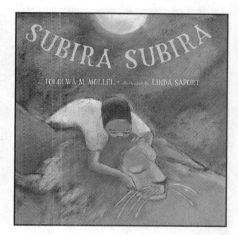

Do It Yourself!

Tololwa Mollel suggests that you choose any character — a king, an ant — and ask yourself, What does this character want? If you do this with a list of ten characters, maybe one will inspire an entire story.

ROBIN MULLER

Born: October 30, 1953, in Toronto, Ontario

Home: Toronto, Ontario

SELECTED TITLES

Mollie Whuppie and the Giant — 1982

Tatterhood — 1984

The Sorcerer's Apprentice — 1985

Little Kay — 1988

The Magic Paintbrush — 1989
(Governor General's Award)

The Nightwood — 1991

Little Wonder — 1994

The Angel Tree — 1997

🎨 *The Happy Prince* — 2001

Badger's New House — 2002

🎨 — *illustrations only*

Ask Robin Muller what he read when he was a boy and he'll tell you, "I read a combination of Shakespeare, *Winnie the Pooh*, *Rupert* annuals and *Freddy the Pig*, which accounts for the twisted person that you meet today, and which probably explains why I can go from something as light and frivolous as *Row, Row, Row Your Boat* to something as dark and intense as *The Magic Paintbrush*."

Robin came to be a children's author and illustrator years after deciding to become an artist. "One reason I started getting into children's books — and now do children's books exclusively — was because I found being a visual artist and dealing with a single static image wasn't satisfying me. I wanted a narrative to the pictures, and children's books were the best

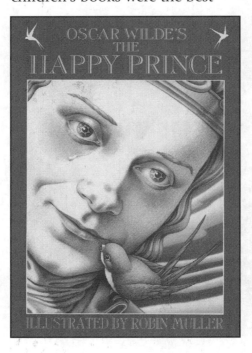

way to include the two."

When he's putting together a new book, Robin works from about nine o'clock in the morning until ten or eleven at night, but he doesn't believe these hours are too long. "As the day progresses, you become more involved in the world on the piece of paper in front of you — it takes on a greater sense of being tangible than the real world." And although Robin does admit that actually getting started in the morning can be difficult, once he gets going, it's equally difficult to drag himself away at night.

TRYING TO REMEMBER

Kids often ask Robin where he gets his ideas, and he says, "I try to remember the things that moved me when I was their age. I try to remember the stories and situations that were a burden to me or helped me get through things, and these are the issues that I like to raise in my stories."

Unlike some illustrators, Robin does not like to get his ideas from the library. "I'm really sloppy with research because I like to be able to use my own visual vocabulary. I pride myself on being someone who actually observes quite well. I take in a lot and I'm always noticing things, but when I sit down to draw, I don't want to have my momentum disturbed by having to run to a book or run to the library or rely on photographs; I just like to be able to draw it. This is why sometimes my drawings are so incredibly inaccurate. When I have to try and figure out how a train works, I fake it. I could never illustrate a textbook for that reason, because I don't really like having to run out and use research material."

When his first book was published, Robin recalls that he wasn't completely happy with his illustrations, largely because creating children's books was so new to him. Now, though, he's less often disappointed with his work. "I can stand back and look at it and think, Robin, you did a good job there. I've covered up the problems better; I've smoothed it out."

> *"You can have chapters of drivel in a novel, but in a picture book it has to be concise, clear and real poetry."*

In an ideal world, Robin would rather have a break before seeing his printed books. "I've always wished that when I finish a book, I wouldn't actually see it for about two years. That way I've completely forgotten it, so when I pick the book up and look at it, it's a fresh experience to me. Instead, from the point in time when I've finished it to when I get it back from the printer, my imagination has actually improved all the illustrations. The colours are brighter and it's better drawn, so that when I see the actual thing — even though it

looks exactly like the illustrations I submitted — I'm disappointed. I think, because I tend to work so obsessively, I really need the obsession to be over before I can come back and really like what I've done."

DO IT YOURSELF!

Robin Muller has had tremendous success using an old toothbrush as a paintbrush. He suggests you try to use something that you would never think to use to make a piece of art. You could, for example, colour with pastels or crayon, then scrape at the surface with an old plastic utensil. Robin's one piece of advice: if you do decide to try his toothbrush idea, don't use your brother's toothbrush unless he's smaller than you are!

ROBERT MUNSCH

Born: June 11, 1945,
in Pittsburgh, Pennsylvania, USA

Home: Guelph, Ontario

SELECTED TITLES

The Paper Bag Princess — 1980

Murmel Murmel Murmel — 1982

Love You Forever — 1986

Thomas's Snowsuit — 1986
(Ruth Schwartz Award)

A Promise Is a Promise — 1988

Something Good — 1990

Stephanie's Ponytail — 1996

Alligator Baby — 1997

We Share Everything — 1999

Playhouse — 2002

Vicky Metcalf Award winner, 1987

When Robert Munsch was working in a childcare centre in 1974, he made up and told his young charges lots and lots of stories. And although he suspected that some of his stories were pretty good, he didn't submit them to a publisher until 1979, when he was working at the University of Guelph. His boss had given him the summer off with orders to publish. "By the end of the summer, I had sent out ten stories to ten different publishers." But only one was interested. That publisher was Annick Press and the story was *Mud Puddle*.

"Most kids know that I put children from out there into my books. So almost all kids ask to be in them." Robert recalls one special book that began with letter he received from an eight-year-old reader. At the time, the girl had just moved to Ontario from Beirut, and in her letter she described to Robert her first Halloween in Canada. Robert was so impressed that he began to correspond with her, and five letters later, the two of them had co-authored *From Far Away*.

PRACTICE MAKES PERFECT

Robert's philosophy must be practice makes perfect, because he fine-tunes his stories (always with an audience) a hundred times or more before he's sure they're ready for his publisher. But Robert doesn't edit on paper.

"The way I do a rewrite is I go out and get an audience. In fact, I don't even think of it as a rewrite. It's just that the story changes very slowly when I'm telling it and telling it and telling it."

> *"I'm like a stand-up comic, reacting to the audience."*

When Robert is ready to try one of his stories on an audience, he refers to a list of schools which have sent him the most imaginative letters and picks one. He prefers to talk to one grade-one or grade-two class at a time when he's refining his material, because if the group is too large, it loses its intimacy and becomes a show. After he's tried his main story on the group, Robert always offers to make up a story for one of the kids in the class.

"It's totally up for grabs, because I generally don't know what I'm going to say. I tend to make up a lot of stories about observable characteristics — hair colour, earrings, purple shoes — because I'm looking at a kid, thinking, What am I going to do now?"

Robert admits that these on-the-spot stories usually aren't that good, but once in a while — as his dozens of books will attest — he comes up with something great. When he thinks he's hit on something, Robert will write to the kid who inspired his story and ask for a photograph, which he then keeps in a file with the story idea until he's ironed out all of the kinks.

It's very important to Robert to acknowledge the kids who inspire his stories. So, if and when he decides to go ahead with a story that's tied to a particular kid, he makes sure that his illustrator uses that child's photograph as reference for one of the characters in the book.

Another way Robert gets ideas is by staying with or visiting the people and places he plans to include in his books. He has, for instance, stayed with a family in a Hutterite colony after corresponding with a number of children who lived there. He's stayed with a wolf hunter in Chesterfield Inlet and a lobster fisherman on Grand Manan Island.

Robert Munsch gets ten thousand fan letters a year from kids. The neatest letters he has ever received have been quilts and flags. The biggest letter he

ever got was four metres tall and was a rolled-up picture of David's father from his book *David's Father*. And the longest letter he ever got was a scroll half a football field long. Needless to say, he was unable to open this one in the house!

DO IT YOURSELF!

If you want to write a story, tell it to three different friends first, then write it down. This will help you work out all of the bugs. It works for Robert Munsch!

KIT PEARSON

Born: April 30, 1947,
in Edmonton, Alberta

Home: Vancouver,
British Columbia

SELECTED TITLES

The Daring Game — 1986

A Handful of Time — 1987
(CLA Book of the Year for Children)

The Sky is Falling — 1989
(CLA Book of the Year for Children,
Geoffrey Bilson Award,
Mr. Christie's Book Award)

The Singing Basket — 1990

Looking at the Moon — 1991

The Lights Go On Again — 1993
(Geoffrey Bilson Award)

Awake and Dreaming — 1996
(Governor General's Award,
Red Cedar Award, Ruth Schwartz Award)

This Land (editor) — 1998

Vicki Metcalf Award winner, 1998

Kit Pearson's life was changed by a book. "When I was twelve, I read *Emily of New Moon* by L.M. Montgomery, which is about a child who wants to be a writer, and is based on Lucy Montgomery's life. After that, I decided I would be a writer, too; it had a profound influence on me."

However, after this revelation, Kit put off a career in writing until she was thirty-five. "I wanted to write all those years, but I was afraid to start, and I didn't know anybody who wrote. Then I became a children's librarian and I was just too busy. But I finally took a year off and went to Simmons College in Boston and got an M.A. in children's literature. Two of the courses I took were in writing for children, and that really got me motivated. I left Simmons determined to start a book."

THE PERFECT AGE

It didn't take long for Kit to decide how old the characters in her novels would be. "I have a very strong memory of being nine to twelve especially. I loved being that age more than I liked being a teenager, so I write about that age." Kit's first book is about going away to boarding school and, although she drew on her own experiences at boarding school when she was a teen, her heroine is eleven and the story is told from a younger girl's point of view.

It can take between one and three years for Kit to write a novel, and during that time she may complete as many as five drafts. Kit doesn't begin with a conventional outline, though; instead, she prefers just to write and see what happens. She creates what she calls a kind of written outline, which includes much of the story, but leaves many gaps for description which will be filled in later. Kit also does a fair bit of planning before she begins, particularly when she's working on a historical novel. *The Sky Is Falling*, for instance, took nearly a year to research.

> *"Once you get an idea planted in your mind, you're very alert to anything you hear about it."*

"My World War II books certainly started with people telling me about World War II. Alice Kane, who's a librarian in Toronto, told me how she used to tell stories to the kids who were evacuated to Canada, and that really got me thinking about these kids. I found out that some of my cousins almost sent their kids to stay with my grandparents, and that my mother knew war guests in Toronto when she was living there during the war."

Kit's interest in the war guests

— children who, for their own safety, were sent to stay with host families in other countries during the Second World War — snowballed until it seemed that she was finding information everywhere. She even took a trip to collect information that would help her create her characters. "I went to England and found a village for them to live in; I talked to people who were kids during the war; and I read newspapers of the time. The only thing I didn't do — and didn't want to do — was talk to people who were actually war guests, because the character of Norah was developing in my mind and I didn't want to write someone else's story.

"I think the most helpful thing was talking to people who were kids during the war, because they supplied me with all kinds of tiny details that I wouldn't have been able to find: what the Christmas decorations were like in 1940, not being able to do up the buttons on your fly if you were a little boy. I think it's the little tiny details that make a story much more real than the historical details."

Despite the long hours research requires, Kit never tires of it. "It was fun to research the World War II books. I think my problem with research is that because I'm a librarian, I love research, and research is a great way of procrastinating. It was very hard to stop doing the research for *The Sky Is Falling*; I could have gone on forever. I kept thinking, I'll just read one more book and then I'll start."

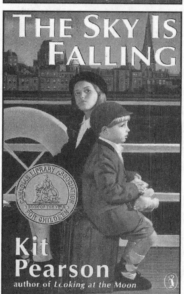

But then, Kit explains, she has always been a reader who couldn't resist just one more book. "When I was a child, I was such an avid reader that I actually ate the books! I used to tear off the bottom right-hand corner or the top right-hand corner and absent-mindedly put it in my mouth and chew it and swallow it. All my childhood books have the corners torn off." This certainly puts a new twist on the expression "devouring a book"!

DO IT YOURSELF!

Kit Pearson's first two novels and her trilogy end with her characters leaving one place and going to another. She suggests you write a letter or a series of letters from Eliza or Patricia or Norah or Gavin to someone they've left behind. What do you think happens to them in their new lives?

STÉPHANE POULIN

Born: December 6, 1961, in Montreal, Quebec

Home: Montreal, Quebec

SELECTED TITLES

*Ah! Belle cité/
A Beautiful City ABC* — 1985

Have You Seen Josephine? — 1986
(Canada Council Prize)

Can You Catch Josephine? — 1987
(Elizabeth Mrazik-Cleaver Award)

*Benjamin and
the Pillow Saga* — 1989
(Governor General's Award)

My Mother's Loves — 1990

Travels for Two — 1991
(Mr. Christie's Book Award)

Family Album — 1991
(Canada Council Prize)

*Poil de serpent
dent d'araignée* — 1996
(Governor General's Award,
Mr. Christie's Book Award)

🎨 *Old Thomas and
the Little Fairy* — 2000

Vicky Metcalf Award winner, 1989

🎨 — *illustrations only*

Stéphane Poulin was first approached to do work as a children's book illustrator and author at an art exhibition in Montreal. Although he still maintains that he cannot write — "I'm not really a writer, and I hate it" — he accepted Tundra's unusual challenge to both write and illustrate a book for kids.

"It was great. My first book was the ABC book *Ah! Belle Cité/A Beautiful City ABC*. They asked me to do the text and the illustrations and the whole conception of the book, which was a very special treat because there was nobody to tell me what to do and how to do it. I was totally free to do what I wanted to do."

After enjoying the experience of handling so many different aspects of the production, Stéphane continues to write his own stories today — because he would rather not wait for stories to come to him, and because as both author and illustrator he has the freedom to draw whatever he likes.

The biggest problem for Stéphane the writer is fleshing out the middle of a story. "All my stories are built like jokes. You have a beginning and a big end, but the middle is not really important. It's tough for me to develop the story and make it longer."

But if Stéphane has trouble with the middle of a book when he's writing, that's where he reaches his stride when he turns into Stéphane the illustrator. Stéphane says that he learns new tricks after he's finished the first few illustrations of a book, and admits that as he nears the end, he often becomes exhausted. So, in order to prevent his books from looking great in the middle and rough on both ends, Stéphane never paints his illustrations in order.

ONE AT A TIME

He's also careful to do his paintings one at a time to avoid feeling as though he were working on an assembly line. And Stéphane has another reason for this approach, too: "In a way, if I work on more than one piece at a time I will repeat the same atmosphere. I prefer to do a complete atmosphere for one, and then when it's over I pass to the second one."

> *"I think if people could work in a place where they could explore their real interests, we would have a beautiful world."*

Stéphane began using oil paints when he was working on his first book. At that time, he and his wife had just had their first son, Gabriel, and were sharing the work of caring for the baby. Oil paints dry slowly, allowing Stéphane to leave his work to change diapers and soothe tears without risking disaster. He's used oils ever since.

When kids ask him which of his books is his favourite, Stéphane tells them, *"Benjamin and the Pillow Saga* is actually the book I prefer because of the spirit of the book. It's very quiet. It's very dark, too. I made that book at a moment where I was happy about my technique. Technically, I was happy."

Stéphane no longer does school visits, however, saying, "It's very difficult because people expect a lot from you when you go to visit, and I'm not an entertainer. I hate to entertain; I feel like I am selling toothpaste. I wish I could be with kids for three or four hours and draw, but I always feel the pressure to read and make kids laugh, which is very artificial."

Stéphane's Josephine books took only about a month to do, but now, as he tries for cleaner, more detailed pictures, Stéphane finds that he needs around eight months to complete a project. Stéphane works only four days a week, saying he doesn't learn much by working all the time. He devotes the rest of his time to his family, explaining, "Being with my children is very, very important."

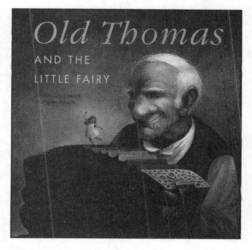

Do It Yourself!

Stéphane Poulin has discovered that pushing yourself to try something new sometimes helps you to develop an existing skill. If you consider yourself to be an artist, try to develop your skill as a writer. You may find that it helps you think more clearly about what to include in your illustrations.

KAREN RECZUCH

Born: July 4, 1956, in Woodstock, Ontario

Home: Acton, Ontario

SELECTED TITLES

The Auction — 1991

Just Like New — 1995
(Amelia Frances Howard-Gibbon Award)

The Dust Bowl — 1996

The Harvest Queen — 1996

Morning on the Lake — 1997

This New Baby — 1998

Melted Star Journey — 1999

Laura: A Childhood Tale of Laura Secord — 2000

The Story of Life on Earth — 2000

Ghost Cat — 2001

An avid reader as a girl, Karen Reczuch doesn't remember ever really being taken with the illustrations in books. For her, the story was the thing. It would take a burning desire for ballet lessons to change all of that.

Karen thinks back: "One Christmas I got a book about ballet dancers. I remember leaving drawings of ballerinas all over the house, hoping my mother might take me for dance classes . . . Instead I got signed up for a painting class at the library.

"As it turned out, the thing I loved to do was draw the pictures of ballerinas. From there I dabbled a short while with being a fashion designer until I discovered I couldn't sew, and again it was just being redirected to the thing I loved to do. It wasn't sewing the dresses but drawing the dresses."

Inspired by "three really wonderful art teachers in high school," Karen went on to study art at Ontario's Sheridan College. And soon after, she encountered Eric Beddows's black-and-white picture book illustrations. Karen says, "It got me thinking really seriously about doing children's books. I hadn't been interested in doing them up until then. I had a lot of black-and-white work that I'd done for my own pleasure, but seeing his work — that it could actually be used as book illustrations . . . "

Karen's first publishing experience was *The Auction*. "That was a formative experience! My first set of thumbnails I think the publisher threw everything out. They said, 'What you have to understand is that you're not telling the same story as the author is. You need to decide what you can add to the story, what else you want to tell.'

> *"The illustrator has to find something else to say other than just repeating what the author has put on the page."*

"The author and the illustrator tell a parallel story. That's quite a neat discovery. But what I found really interesting — and a little shocking: when I came in with my final thumbnails, there were whole passages in the text that just got cut because I was 'saying it' in the pictures. It's something that I've taken with me since my first book. You really are doing this together."

A TREEHOUSE IN A LUMBER MILL

Karen shares space in a converted lumber mill in Glen Williams, Ontario, with about thirty other artists and artisans, including glassblowers, potters and painters. Her studio is on the second floor with windows that come down almost to the floor, giving full show to the trees outside.

About half the time Karen spends on each project is devoted to research, while the other half is spent drawing. She begins with simple line sketches, then finds someone to model for the photographs she will refer to for her final illustrations.

She also tries to visit the location of the story, if possible. "Even doing a book like *Melted Star Journey*, which mostly takes place in a car, there were hours of just studying how a raindrop runs down a car window or how my kids get all tangled up together. It's a lot of just looking at everyday things that you don't normally pay attention to."

Karen believes strongly in the idea that every story has a "right illustrator," and as a result has turned down a couple of projects over the years. "They were wonderful texts, but when I was

reading through them the pictures I was seeing in my head weren't my pictures. I could see them being done by a different artist. It's quite delightful to walk through a store a year later and see the story that you thought somebody else could do better and say, Yeah, I was right!"

DO IT YOURSELF!

Karen Reczuch appreciates how important it is for the author and the illustrator to complement each other's work by telling different aspects of the same story. Try it with a friend: after one of you has written a story, let the other tell a different side of the story in pictures.

BARBARA REID

Born: November 16, 1957,
in Toronto, Ontario

Home: Toronto, Ontario

SELECTED TITLES

🎨 *The New Baby Calf* — 1984

🎨 *Have You Seen Birds?* — 1986
(Elizabeth Mrazik-Cleaver Award, Canada
Council Prize, Ruth Schwartz Award)

🎨 *Sing a Song of
Mother Goose* — 1987

🎨 *Effie* — 1990

Two by Two — 1992
(Elizabeth Mrazik-Cleaver Award)

🎨 *Gifts* — 1994
(Amelia Frances Howard-Gibbon Award)

The Party — 1997
(Amelia Frances Howard-Gibbon Award,
Governor General's Award)

Fun With Modelling Clay — 1998

The Golden Goose — 2000

Zoe (series) — 1992, 2002
(Mr. Christie's Book Award)

🎨 — illustrations only

Barbara Reid has been playing with Plasticine ever since she was in elementary school, where she used it to create models for practically every project she was assigned. A particularly memorable piece for Barbara was a model she made of an entire maple sugar bush!

For Barbara, the decision to earn her living as an artist was made in an instant. Barbara had never planned to become a professional illustrator: at her high school, art was considered to be something of a joke. But she abruptly changed her mind when, on career day, a couple of students from the Ontario College of Art came to speak at her school. Barbara admits that at first she was drawn into the presentation merely because the presenters happened to be "really cute guys," but it was the thought that she could do what she loved for a living that sold her on the

idea. And so, in grade thirteen, risking ridicule from her peers, Barbara Reid enrolled at the Ontario College of Art.

There, Barbara's favourite area of study was art history. In fact, she's still interested in the puzzle of who an artist really is — looking in every piece for clues about the artist and about what he or she is trying to say. In her own work, Barbara says that she is usually making fun of something that is serious or pompous; she thinks of herself as a cartoonist.

EARLY DISAPPOINTMENTS

Barbara's first publishing experiences weren't as exciting as her current efforts. She did a lot of textbooks and other small jobs to help her pay the bills. Sometimes these projects were discouraging because the paper and printing weren't the best (authors and illustrators who are just starting out often work on small, cheaply produced books until they gain some experience), and she felt that her artwork never looked as good on the printed page as it did in her original. In particular, she found the colours dull or inaccurate, and it was often disappointing to see these unchangeable mistakes. Barbara has, with time, learned not to take these disappointments to heart. She tries to look at her finished books as a consumer would, and that — coupled with the better paper and printing techniques that are available to her today — makes her feel a lot happier about her publishing experiences.

Kids often ask Barbara, How do you get the Plasticine into the book? She explains that the Plasticine isn't actually in the book. Instead, Barbara's Plasticine art is photographed and it's those photos that appear on the printed page. The photographs are vital to the way the book will look, so Barbara and her photographer husband spend a great deal of time setting up the lights and framing the shots.

The other question young artists ask Barbara is, "Where do you get all of those colours of Plasticine?" Barbara doesn't buy all of the colours you see in her books; she mixes them. She admits that some of the colours available are really dull, so she "cheats" to make them seem brighter. She puts yellows beside blues, employing all of the tricks of contrasting colours, which, she explains, is another technique she learned at art college.

"If you want to draw something, you have to look at it."

The first time Barbara had the opportunity to illustrate and write a picture book, she learned a lot in the process. "Writing is hard work," explains Barbara. "Illustrating is enjoyable hard work." Barbara confesses that her experience taught her that she prefers to work on the

illustrations only, spending her time reshaping an idea or solving the problem of illustrating someone else's tale. For jobs like those, Barbara exclaims, "Writers are my heroes! I'm just decorating the story."

Barbara's illustrations are big and heavy. They can weigh anywhere between two and an incredible seven kilograms and must be stored individually, so Barbara packs each into its own pizza box for safekeeping. Needless to say, Barbara doesn't have enough room at home to take all of the "pages" of her books out and look at them together, so she really enjoys having an art show once in a while. And because she doesn't have enough room at home to keep every single piece, Barbara sells her art after her books are printed, saying "I'm more attached to the books than I am to the art."

DO IT YOURSELF!

Here's an idea from Barbara Reid, art-history buff: Do a portrait of someone, and include in the portrait something that tells about that person's activities or interests. For example, if the person has a pet rabbit, he or she could be holding a carrot in the portrait.

BARBARA SMUCKER

Born: September 1, 1915, in Newton, Kansas, USA

Home: Bluffton, Ohio, USA

SELECTED TITLES

Henry's Red Sea — 1955

Underground to Canada — 1977

Days of Terror — 1979
(Canada Council Prize,
Ruth Schwartz Award)

Amish Adventure — 1982

White Mist — 1985

Jacob's Little Giant — 1987

Incredible Jumbo — 1990

Garth and the Mermaid — 1992

Selina and the
Bear Paw Quilt — 1995

Selina and the Shoo-Fly Pie — 1998

Vicky Metcalf Award winner, 1988

Barbara Smucker recalls one of her first writing experiences: "My best friend and I wrote a novel together in longhand. It was a romance about a prince and a princess. We were too shy to let anyone else read it. I remember going out to the field with a shovel, digging a hole for the book, then putting a rock on it to remember the place." The book was not there when she returned fifty years later to dig it up. An apartment building was in its place.

> *"I think of myself as a Canadian writer."*

Barbara studied to become a journalist and later worked for a local newspaper, but her next significant publishing experience didn't come for many years. "I heard the story from a man who was visiting our home. Our children were very small at that time, and they listened so intently to this story that I thought it really should be written for children and not be just an incident that was recorded in the newspaper. So, I wrote it with a seven- or eight-year-old boy in mind — Henry, I called him." The book was *Henry's Red Sea*.

Barbara then approached her Mennonite church's publisher. "It was one of the first children's books that they published. And I was pretty excited about it. I'd written newspaper stories and short stories, but I'd never had a book published. I remember getting it in the mail one day when it was finished and I was so excited and nervous I could hardly hold it. It's a very thrilling event in a writer's life to publish a first book."

In 1969, Barbara and her husband moved north to Waterloo, Ontario, where they lived and worked for three decades. Barbara published many fine works of fiction during those years, and she has long been regarded as one of Canada's top authors.

AN EDITOR'S SUGGESTIONS

The publishing experience has always been an enjoyable one for Barbara. "I've been very fortunate to have two excellent editors; they've been very knowledgeable about the book field and have been very, very helpful. I tell them what I'm working on, then I try to complete the whole manuscript. When I'm writing, I realize it isn't the way it's going to be when it's finished. My editors have made outstanding suggestions — sometimes I've used them and sometimes I haven't. They haven't made me feel that I'm compelled to change my manuscripts the way they want them to be.

"Most of the books I write for young people are called historical fiction. They are stories about true, important and dramatic events in history, and I have them happen to imaginary boys and girls and their families."

Barbara has always found it helpful to read her stories aloud. "Once I was in a writers' group, where we read things aloud to each other. You could only be in this writers' group if you had published, so they were serious writers. And that was helpful, too, because no one hesitated about being highly critical. Sometimes it was difficult to be there — sometimes you almost hated to read your material — but it was really helpful. I do think the input of another person is important for a writer. At least it has been for me."

Barbara has visited schools all over Canada and is amazed at the number of kids she has met who have been new to this country. She marvels at the great work they and

their teachers are doing with books, and she encourages them all to look back into their own family histories for story ideas.

Do It Yourself!

Barbara Smucker's books are based on true stories that she has heard. She suggests you interview your grandmother or grandfather or some older person you know and do a little story research. Ask what their lives were like when they were your age. What did they wear? What did they study? What sports or games did they play? What important world events were happening then?

MAXINE TROTTIER

Born: May 3, 1950,
in Grosse Pointe Farms, Michigan

Home: Port Stanley, Ontario

SELECTED TITLES

The Tiny Kite of Eddie Wing —1995
(CLA Book of the Year for Children)

Heartsong — 1997

Prairie Willow — 1998

Claire's Gift — 1999
(Mr. Christie's Book Award)

Dreamstones — 1999

Flags — 1999

One Is Canada — 1999

A Circle of Silver — 2000

*Laura: A Childhood Tale
of Laura Secord* — 2000

Native Crafts — 2000

As a kid, Maxine Trottier loved to draw. She played hockey on frozen puddles, built treehouses and read and read and read. But she did not write. There were no writers in Maxine's family when she was growing up. There were plenty of storytellers, but their stories were always told in French, a language she has never spoken or understood. It would be years before she would consider herself a writer.

Maxine declares, "I'm a great believer in timing. You can only plan so much of your life and then something will happen to you . . . "

One summer, Maxine was at a party and someone lost a heart-shaped balloon. It floated over the fence and off into the neighbourhood. Someone exclaimed, 'Now that balloon is going to land in someone's backyard and make them very happy.' And so the idea for her first book, *The Big Heart*, was born.

A grade-two teacher, Maxine was forty years old and about to embark on a second career, this time as a writer. Convinced that she couldn't possibly write a story and get it published on her own, she worked with a friend, and together they devised a highly specialized method for selecting a publisher: alphabetically. Ten days after they submitted it to Annick Press, they received word that their story had been accepted.

Maxine grins, "They were my foot in the door and I've always been very grateful to them."

Once published, Maxine was hooked. She likens her experience to being a meteorite travelling through space and then suddenly being pulled into a gravitational field. There would be no pulling away from this new kind of work. "I stopped fighting the idea that I must write. Doubts? No. I am a writer."

> *"The world is changing and electronic publishing is part of that, but there will always be a lap waiting for a book."*

Success did not follow right away. Maxine remembers, "After *The Big Heart*, I wrote a number of dreadful stories. I didn't have my voice as a writer yet — not until I wrote *The Tiny Kite of Eddie Wing*. Right then, with that book, every single thing changed and I realized how I was supposed to write for the rest of my life. It was almost effortless once I opened myself up to it."

Maxine has saved every one of the "hundreds" of rejection letters mailed to her over the years. "Sometimes they hurt and sometimes they were encouraging, but I did not ever let them become discouraging. I look at them every once in a while and I think that's how much work it took. If you want something badly enough, you have to be relentless. I don't consider it a waste of time. It was just something I had to go through."

A Boat and Two Dogs

Although she has a studio at home, almost all of Maxine's books have been written at least in part on her boat. When a book calls for it, Maxine has been know to weigh anchor near a historical site about which she is writing, allowing her to work on location in a way that few authors can. She writes on her laptop, either below deck or, when the sun shines, outside under the awning in the cockpit.

"I have always been a bookish sort, from the time before I could read. The smell of old books and the feel of them got into my blood at a very early age. I like music, books, dragonflies, sailing,

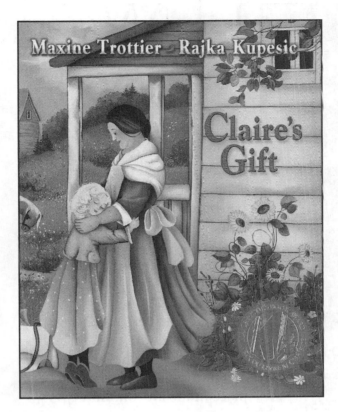

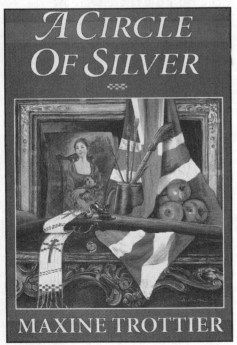

history, discovering new things about Canada and the people who live here. I am everywhere in my books, particularly if they have anything to do with sailing.

"You write about what you know and love, about what moves you and — you hope — will move others."

Do It Yourself!

Take a tip from Maxine Trottier: when you are searching for a topic to write about, look at something familiar in a different way. Leave your thoughts open to possibilities. What sort of place would Canada be if France instead of England had won the Seven Years' War, for instance?

IAN WALLACE

Born: March 31, 1950,
in Niagara Falls, Ontario

Home: Toronto, Ontario

SELECTED TITLES

*Chin Chiang and the
Dragon's Dance* — 1984
(Amelia Frances Howard-Gibbon Award)

🎨 *Very Last First Time* — 1985

Morgan the Magnificent — 1987

🎨 *The Name of the Tree* — 1989
(Mr. Christie's Book Award,
Elizabeth Mrazik-Cleaver Award)

🎨 *The Mummer's Song* — 1993

🎨 *Hansel and Gretel* — 1994

🎨 *Sarah and the People
of Sand River* — 1996

A Winter's Tale — 1997

Boy of the Deeps — 1999

Duncan's Way — 2000

🎨 — illustrations only

From the age of four, Ian Wallace was well on his way to becoming an artist. "I always loved to draw and it wasn't always in the places I should have been drawing, like paper. It was on bedroom walls and even in the covers of books."

When he was thirteen, Ian decided to become an artist in earnest, even though, at the time, he didn't quite know what the life of an artist entailed. He carried that desire right through to college, where he began to search for his own particular place in the art community.

> *"I need the quiet solitude of time to write and illustrate, but I also have to be that gregarious performer who goes out and shakes and rattles and rolls kids and hangs them from the ceiling."*

"I felt the education I was getting at college when I was in graphic design was too narrow and so focused on design it didn't take in the whole creative process. So I began to move out and embrace all the disciplines possible within that college, and upon graduation I was a master of many things, but a master of nothing. *But* I had learned to

think, and that, to me, is the bottom line of all creativity. That sounds rather clichéd, but I learned that all creative activity begins in the head first and the hands second. Before I went to art school, I thought it all began in the hand. I didn't imagine that I would have to use my brain or think about what I was doing and why I was doing it."

THE RIGHT PLACE AT THE RIGHT TIME

After graduation, Ian had what he describes as the happy luck of finding himself in the right place at the right time, which happened to be the local student bar. "Sitting to my right was one of the founding members of Kids Can Press. She was talking that evening about the press and what it was trying do, and how there were no books in this country for kids, published by Canadian writers and illustrators. I became intrigued and interested in the idea of working there for the summer. I thought it would be an interesting way to pass two months but realized, within three weeks of being hired on that project, not only did I want to draw, but I wanted to write, too."

Over time, Ian has learned that although picture books are relatively short, each requires a great deal of work. "In terms of quality, I think that you really can only produce one, hopefully fine, book each year. I would be really hard pressed to go through all the things I need to do to in a shorter span of time."

One of the time-consuming things Ian feels he must do when he writes is, as he describes it, "get under the skin of those characters," fine-tuning his work until every one is just right. For instance, his revisions for *Chin Chiang and the Dragon's Dance* were so extensive that the stack of manuscript pages stood about thirty centimetres high and the paper weighed about seven kilograms. Yet there are only 160 lines of text in the finished book!

Ian says, "You have to have the courage and the patience and the tenacity to know when to go back to that story, to know when to put it away, to know when to take it out, to know when to drop portions and passages and themes and elements that are not working, when to draw back, and when to come in like gangbusters."

One of Ian's biggest worries as an artist is correctness. "In books like *Chin Chiang and the Dragon's Dance* and *Very Last First Time*, I was dealing with completely different cultures, different landscapes, different histories and different societies. The kind of responsibility that was on me was enormous because as Newfoundlanders would say, I'm 'from away.' Even when I was doing my book *The Mummer's Song*, I felt somewhat nervous about being 'from away,' and that's always a nice emotion to feel because it keeps you on your toes and you make sure with

every ounce of your energy that the story is told with the dignity and respect due that culture."

Some years ago Ian was asked if he might consider doing a version of *Hansel and Gretel*. His initial response was "no" because, as far as he could see, there already were classic versions in existence. Why reinvent the wheel? Ian changed his mind, though, when his editor convinced him that for each generation there is a new version that readers embrace. His editor also imparted a few wise words that apply to more than this project, telling Ian "you have something to say with everything that you do."

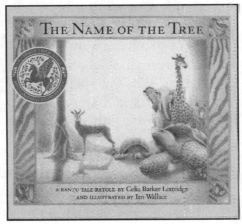

DO IT YOURSELF!

Ian Wallace suggests you experiment with different media (paints, pencils, markers, crayons, etc.). Do an illustration, then draw the same picture again, this time using a different medium. How does changing the medium change the look of the picture?

ERIC WALTERS

Born: March 3, 1957, in Toronto, Ontario

Home: Mississauga, Ontario

SELECTED TITLES

Stand Your Ground — 1994

Stars — 1996
(Silver Birch Award)

Trapped in Ice — 1997
(Silver Birch Award)

War of the Eagles — 1998
(Ruth Schwartz Award)

The Hydrofoil Mystery — 1999

Tiger by the Tail — 1999

The Bully Boys — 2000

The Money Pit Mystery — 2000

Rebound — 2000

Northern Exposures — 2001

Eric Walters is a busy man. He's a grade-five teacher, but he also works part time as a crisis social worker at Mississauga's Credit Valley Hospital. He's a soccer coach and a basketball coach. He's a father of three. He likes jazz and takes saxophone lessons. And he's also a very successful author who writes five books a year. How does one person do so much? Eric laughs, "I don't sleep a lot. I just keep moving."

A very disciplined writer, Eric uses nearly every free moment he can find. "I write during recesses, lunch hours, at seven in the morning, at eleven at night. I write whenever I have time. Once when I was driving back from a school presentation, a grain truck flipped and I was trapped on the highway. Everyone was pretty upset. In that hour and twenty minutes when we couldn't move, I wrote seven pages. My upset was when they made us move again!"

Writing quickly does not mean writing badly for Eric Walters. His writing has charmed thousands of readers, in four languages.

All of this from a man who started writing books only six years ago. "What happened is this. I had a class that was not particularly into either reading or writing so I wrote a story for them and I put them in. I set it in the school where I was teaching, and I put their names and characters in the story. That book became *Stand Your Ground.*"

Eric wrote that first book to get his class excited about reading and writing, but he didn't think about sending it to a publisher until his class convinced him to submit it — they thought it was better than a lot of the books in the school library.

> *"Editors really make you look good. I listen to editors. They know their part of the job, and I've never had an editor who didn't improve a book dramatically. It's kind of like having a writing lesson."*

"I got lucky!" Eric remembers. "I picked six publishers and sent it off. I got five rejection letters."

To date, every novel Eric has written has been accepted for publication. That's twenty-two contracted books in six years!

Eric explains that a critical part of the writing process comes about in the establishment of the writer/editor team. "I was told I could get obnoxious after the fifth book, but I haven't done it yet. You've got to accept that people know what they're doing. At times I'll ask for clarification, and at times I've said, I don't like that. I think if you treat people well and don't fight them over details, they aren't going to fight you when you want things to stand."

Eric enjoys his job — he likes the fact that he actually gets paid to tell stories. "It just gives you an excuse to play. Because all writing is is being playful."

Part of the fun for Eric is getting to do the hands-on research that some of his stories require. He spent days in a wheelchair while researching *Rebound,* and touched things that belonged to Alexander Graham Bell while working on *The Hydrofoil Mystery.*

STORIES JUST JUMP OUT AT YOU

Eric draws on his own experiences when he's looking for ideas, shaping events to suit the book he plans to write. This is how his book *Northern Exposures* came about.

"It's about this kid named Kevin Spreekmeester who enters a Capture Mississauga Photo Contest and wins, and they send him to Churchill, Manitoba, to photograph polar bears with a *National Geographic* photographer. The reason I'm writing that story is I have a friend named Kevin Spreekmeester who entered the Capture Mississauga Photo Contest and won and was sent to Churchill, Manitoba, to photograph polar bears with a *National Geographic* photographer. What I did was make Kevin fourteen instead of forty, and I gave him back his hair. He was very grateful."

In keeping with his goal to reach as many young readers as

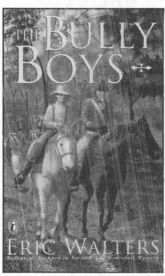

possible, Eric writes everything from first chapter books for beginning readers to historical and contemporary fiction for older readers, each of which he sends to different editors. And although he tries to alternate projects so he always has something on the go with each of his five publishers, he feels it's important not to force an idea to become a particular kind of book.

Says Eric, "Stories know what they should be."

DO IT YOURSELF!

Eric Walters's advice to young writers is the same he would give to an aspiring pro basketball player: Practise and listen to your coaches (in most cases these are your teachers). And look at how the pros do it: read other people's books and see what works and what doesn't. You learn from the people you read.

ERIC WILSON

Born: November 24, 1940,
in Ottawa, Ontario

Home: Victoria, British Columbia

SELECTED TITLES

Murder on the Canadian — 1976

The Ghost of Lunenburg Manor — 1981

Spirit of the Rainforest — 1984

The Green Gables Detectives — 1987

Code Red at the Supermall — 1988

The Ice Diamond Quest — 1990

The Prairie Dog Conspiracy — 1992

The St. Andrews Werewolf — 1993

The Inuk Mountie Adventure — 1995

The Emily Carr Mystery — 2001

Eric Wilson began his writing career when he was a teacher. "I was working with grade-eight students in BC — kids who didn't like to read at all and didn't seem to know much about Canada. That's what gave me my two principal goals, which were to write about Canada and to write books that would get kids into reading."

Over the years, Eric has discovered exactly the best way to develop books that accomplish just those goals. "I select a location and go and live there, then try and incorporate into my stories as many of my own personal experiences as possible."

WRITER ON LOCATION

For example, in preparation for his book *The Inuk Mountie Adventure*, in which the character Tom Austen is on an exchange trip from Winnipeg to Gjoa Haven, Eric joined a group of junior high school students on a winter exchange in that very same arctic town. They went out with dog-sled teams and built igloos, and Eric made a particular effort to get to know the people and their community. "Like the students, I was billeted with a family and so we got to eat caribou and that sort of thing. All those experiences [went] into my story."

Eric also carries a tape recorder on these excursions to dictate notes and to record as much of the moment as he can.

"For example, when we were out with the dog-sled teams on the ice, I had the microcassette with me. I was muttering into it as we bumped and banged across the ice so that I could get the actual sounds of the dogs and the sled runners in the snow." He wanted to capture every detail of that thrilling ride and try to reproduce it in his story.

"I don't have children, but I like to think of my readers as my kids."

"That, essentially, is what the research is; it's going to a real place and writing about it. That's why when I talk to kids in schools, I always say, If you're going to do a story, begin by writing about some place that you know, namely your own neighbourhood or your own town."

When his field work is complete, Eric takes all that raw data home, where he spends between two and four months assembling it, thinking about his characters and sorting related information into separate files on his computer.

"For example, I'll have a scene that takes place at the school in Gjoa Haven, and so all the research that I did at the school I'll assemble in one file in my computer. Then when I come to do the actual writing, I'll go through that material and pick out what I think is the most interesting and telling information."

When it finally comes time to write the first draft of his new story, Eric will do the same thing he always does when he's writing: he'll cut himself off from every distraction. "When I'm going to be writing, I switch off the phone, hang a Do Not Disturb sign on the door of my apartment and close all of the curtains so that I cut off my beautiful view of the Pacific Ocean and the mountains. The only light on in my apartment is a little tiny light glowing over my computer keyboard, so it's like a dark little cave. I like to be in that cave, so that when I'm writing my story, I'm in Gjoa Haven rather than in Victoria."

It takes Eric about two months to complete his first draft, which he then prints out ten times for what he describes as ten really important editors — five girls and five boys in grades four through eight from a school in Victoria. "They take the story home with them and they keep a diary. At the end of each chapter, they stop and write down the answers to several questions for me, including who they think the villain is and why, because this is a test-read for the clues." Eric also asks them to let him know where he's used dated language and where they think the story gets boring. "In other words, those ten kids read the story on behalf of all the kids who will read it as a book."

Then, of course, Eric works on rewrites with his editor from

HarperCollins, and after another couple of months of work, his manuscript is finally ready for his publisher. Not a bad system, really. Since Eric's books have been wildly popular with thousands of kids across Canada and as far away as Spain and Japan, one can't help but agree that he is indeed achieving his goals!

DO IT YOURSELF!

Accurate description is very important to Eric Wilson, so he's always very careful to describe not only what is seen but also what can be heard, smelled, touched and tasted. Try to remember to include descriptions of all of the things your characters sense the next time you write a story.

JANET WILSON

Born: November 20, 1952, in Toronto, Ontario

Home: Eden Mills, Ontario

SELECTED TITLES

🎨 *Daniel's Dog* — 1990

🎨 *Jess Was the Brave One* — 1991

🎨 *Tiger Flowers* — 1994

🎨 *Selina and the Bear Paw Quilt* — 1994
(Elizabeth Mrazik-Cleaver Award)

🎨 *In Flanders Fields* — 1995
(Information Book Award, Red Cedar Award)

🎨 *At Grandpa's Sugar Bush* — 1997

🎨 *Amazing Grace* — 1997

🎨 *Selina and the Shoo-Fly Pie* — 1998

Imagine That! — 2000

🎨 *Anna's Goat* — 2000

🎨 — illustrations only

Although she worked on her school's yearbook design and was co-creator of a special mural which is still on display in her old junior high, Janet Wilson never had the confidence to take her work as an artist seriously.

"Looking back on it, the ability was always there. I would do things and they'd look pretty good, but I always thought, Well, that was just a fluke, whereas somebody else would say, It's good because *I'm* good."

Janet believes that without encouragement and confidence, the only way to succeed is to change your attitude. And that's exactly what she did when, at the age of twenty-nine, she went to college for the first time to become an artist.

Encouraged by friends who were already professional illustrators, Janet was determined to make as much of this learning experience as she could. "I had maturity enough to know that when I graduated, I had to be as good as the people who were out there already. So I made a real effort to learn and improve on each assignment. I had a drive because I knew what professional standards were."

Success came when Janet was approached by the art director at Scholastic to do her first picture book. "I had no idea when I started it what I was getting myself into." Janet had already had an easy time doing educational books, requiring twelve pictures each, and she thought that the thirty-two pages of illustrations required for a picture book would be just as easy to do.

STARTING OVER

But Janet soon realized that storybooks are far more complicated than that; there has to be a common style throughout. "I got into the book — I think I had done about five pages — and I didn't like it. I thought, I can't carry this through the whole book! Each picture was so different. I had to change to a style that would be suitable for every page; so, I started over. I went through about four pages and I started to panic again. I thought, No, this isn't working either. I ended up starting that book over three times!"

> *"If it's not working right from the beginning, you're only repairing it. You need to make a good start."*

Today, Janet doesn't let a problem go that far, but instead makes a clean start by breaking her board over her knee to prevent her from fiddling with it. "I start more pictures over than you can even imagine. I can spend two weeks on a painting that has to be handed in in two

SELINA AND THE
BEAR PAW QUILT

BARBARA SMUCKER
Illustrated by JANET WILSON

In
Flanders Fields

The Story of the Poem by John McCrae

Linda Granfield • Illustrated by Janet Wilson

days, and if I don't like it, I'll start over. It's sickening, but it always looks better. Always!"

So how does Janet know when she's on track? "It's hard to describe, but every book tells you what to do; it speaks to you so that — in my books anyway — you'll notice that they aren't all the same style. I really feel that the book dictates how it's going to look. I wasn't listening to that in the beginning, but now I listen to it. I know more and more, as I do them, how to do them."

A particular favourite of Janet's, and a perfect example of a book dictating its own style, is her book *Selina and the Bear Paw Quilt*. She painted all of the pictures on canvas so the borders could be quilted, and she did a lot of research. "It takes place in the Mennonite community in Kitchener. So I went there and I spoke to Mennonites. I went to a quilting bee, I went to a museum and I sort of immersed myself into the culture. There are so many things you have to think about. Like, for instance, What

would a little girl wear to bed? Would she have a nightgown? Would she wear a hat? Would she tie the ribbons in her hair in bows? Or would they be strings? All these things you don't necessarily need to write about, but if it's in a picture and it's not accurate, people are going to notice."

Janet takes her work very seriously, often working long hours to perfect it. But she says she loves every minute of it. "I hadn't really thought about doing children's books, but once I did it, I was hooked. I never looked back and I never wanted to do anything else after that."

DO IT YOURSELF!

Here's an art activity from Janet Wilson. On a piece of paper, make three unconnected squiggles. Then, pass your paper to someone else, and challenge that person to join the lines to create a picture.

WERNER ZIMMERMANN

Born: November 20, 1951, in Wörgl, Austria

Home: Lion's Head, Ontario

SELECTED TITLES

🎨 *Farmer Joe's Hot Day* — 1987

🎨 *Henny Penny* — 1989

Alphonse Knows:
A Circle Is Not a Valentine — 1990

🎨 *Finster Frets* — 1992

🎨 *In My Backyard* — 1992

🎨 *Whatever You Do, Don't Go*
Near That Canoe! — 1996

🎨 *Farmer Joe Baby-Sits* — 1997

🎨 *Each One Special* — 1998

🎨 *Brave Highland Heart* — 1999

Snow Day! — 1999

🎨 — illustrations only

Werner Zimmermann recalls being a poor reader when he was a kid, and he admits that for years this caused him to stay away from books. He also remembers not having many places to play in the town where he grew up, and finally turning to books as an escape. "I don't think I tweaked into books until grade six. It was a horrible, boring summer and I read these really neat adventure books by Enid Blyton. Here were kids on a sailboat who had real adventures — they had everything in the summer that I didn't."

"When people ask me how I got into books I have to say, Face first."

Werner's introduction to making books was also a little unusual. It didn't come out of a discussion with a publisher, but rather from a discussion with a kindergarten teacher. "The first book I did was because my son was in kindergarten and he was having problems reading — he has the same difficulties with words that I do. We had him in French immersion, and I went to the teacher asking for books that we could read to him. She pointed out that everything was written for kids who'd spent their first five years at home speaking French. So, I said, 'I'm an artist; is there something I could do?'"

That teacher seized the opportunity and asked Werner to do a Valentine's Day book about shapes. And so began the first draft of *A Circle Is Not a Valentine* and Werner Zimmermann's career in children's books.

Werner has a great respect for his young readers and prefers to create stories he knows they'll enjoy, rather than those with an obvious preachy moral. He is trying, perhaps, to reach kids who, like himself, aren't drawn to books right away. In fact, he confesses that he often gets so serious about his work that he becomes distracted and dips his paintbrush in his coffee and drinks his paint water!

Werner is just as serious about sketching his subject matter, and he does this for days, long before he ever takes out his watercolours and pencil crayons. He recalls one sketching outing when, as he prepared his drawings for *Henny Penny*, Werner learned the difference between private chickens and public chickens. "Public chickens just act like chickens. Private chickens have a whole different kind of personality. I sat in a chicken coop and drew them there. The farmer looked at me as if I was nuts! It's neat collecting the little stuff to put into a book when you're really left alone to do it."

A PIG ON AN ESCALATOR

On another sketching outing, Werner recalls working on the

pictures for *Farmer Joe Goes to the City.* "While drawing the scene on the escalators, I was asked to leave a prominent department store because they thought I was sketching the new and secret display being set up — as if I were a spy for the rivals. It was rather sad to leave, because the pig was having such a grand time on the escalator!

"I loved doing that book because I experience the same thing as Joe every time I need to shop for a gift. I am envious of him only because he got to take his animals. I can think of no greater fun than to take a cow, a pig and some chickens to a mall."

Werner is always striving to make his paintings better, although he admits to doubting he'll ever be completely satisfied with a project. "I admire those people who say, This is the way it was meant to be, and this is the way I've done it, and there it is — it's finished and it's done right."

For Werner, it isn't that cut and dried. He advises new illustrators not to expect the work to be easy, and to be willing to slug it out even when people are telling you it isn't worth the effort. "If you want to do it, then do it. Don't let people talk you out of it. Take good advice, but ignore the naysayers."

Do It Yourself!

Werner Zimmermann says the secret to putting life into your drawings is to draw people and animals from the inside out. For this, stick figures are really valuable. He says they help an artist learn a lot about movement and suggests that you use them as your beginning point, adding features when you've established where your characters will bend and how they will move.

AWARDS

As you read through this book, you will notice references to major national awards that many of the authors and illustrators have received. Many have received more awards than are listed here, including international awards, but there simply wasn't enough space to fit them all in.

Following is a brief description of each of Canada's major national children's book awards.

THE AMELIA FRANCES HOWARD-GIBBON ILLUSTRATOR'S AWARD

Awarded annually by the Canadian Library Association (CLA) for the best illustrated children's book. The illustrator must be Canadian and the book published in Canada, and the text must be worthy of its illustrations.

ARTHUR ELLIS AWARD, JUVENILE LITERATURE

Awarded annually by the Crime Writers of Canada to the author of the best juvenile crime fiction or mystery novel. The author may be resident in Canada or a Canadian residing abroad.

THE CANADA COUNCIL CHILDREN'S LITERATURE PRIZE

In 1986 this award was renamed the Governor General's Award for Children's Literature. See description at right.

CLA BOOK OF THE YEAR AWARD FOR CHILDREN

Awarded annually by the CLA for the best work of creative literature (fiction, drama or poetry) for children. The author must be Canadian and the book published in Canada.

CLA YOUNG ADULT CANADIAN BOOK AWARD

Awarded annually by the CLA for the best work of creative literature (fiction, drama or poetry) for young adults. The author must be Canadian and the book published in Canada.

ELIZABETH MRAZIK-CLEAVER AWARD

Awarded annually by the Canadian section of the International Board on Books for Young People (IBBY) to the best Canadian illustrator of a picture book published in Canada. Established in 1985 from a bequest by children's book illustrator Elizabeth Mrazik-Cleaver.

THE GEOFFREY BILSON AWARD FOR HISTORICAL FICTION FOR YOUNG PEOPLE

Awarded annually by The Canadian Children's Book Centre to a Canadian author of an outstanding work of historical fiction for young people. Established in 1988 in memory of historian and children's author Geoffrey Bilson.

GOVERNOR GENERAL'S LITERARY AWARDS, CHILDREN'S LITERATURE

Awarded annually by the Canada Council for best text in an English-language children's book, best text in a French-language book, best illustrations in an English-language book and best illustrations in a French-language book. Before 1987 this award was known as The Canada Council Children's Literature Prize.

HACKMATACK CHILDREN'S CHOICE BOOK AWARD

Three awards are presented each spring for best fiction, non-fiction and French-language books. A selection committee chooses thirty outstanding Canadian books to be read and voted on by students in grades 4 to 6 across the Atlantic provinces.

INFORMATION BOOK AWARD

Awarded annually by the Children's Literature Roundtables of Canada for the best Canadian non-fiction book for children. The Roundtables also honour at least one runner-up book annually.

MR. CHRISTIE'S™ BOOK AWARDS

Six award winners (three English-language, three French-language) are chosen annually by a panel of children's book specialists in the following categories: best Canadian book for children ages seven and under, for children ages eight to eleven and for children ages twelve to sixteen. Sponsored by the Nabisco Biscuit and Snacks Division of Kraft Foods Inc.

NORMA FLECK AWARD

Awarded annually by the Canadian Children's Book Centre for the best non-fiction book for children, written and illustrated by Canadians. Established in 1999 in memory of early-literacy advocate Norma Fleck.

RUTH SCHWARTZ CHILDREN'S BOOK AWARD

Two prizes, one for best picture book and one for best middle grade/young adult book, are awarded annually by the Ontario Arts Council to Canadian children's authors. The shortlist is selected by the Canadian Booksellers Association and voted on by a jury of schoolchildren. Established in memory of Toronto bookstore proprietor Ruth Schwartz.

SILVER BIRCH AWARDS

Administered by the Ontario Library Association (OLA), this reader's choice award program recognizes one fiction and one non-fiction book. Books selected by the award committee are read and voted on by students in grades 4 to 6 across Ontario.

RED MAPLE AWARD

A reader's choice award administered by the OLA. Grade 7 to 9 students across Ontario read a selection of ten outstanding Canadian young adult novels, and vote for the winner.

RED CEDAR BOOK AWARDS

These awards are presented annually to the authors of one fiction and one non-fiction book, voted on by readers in grades 4 to 7 across British Columbia. Authors must have resided in Canada for at least two years.

VICKY METCALF BODY OF WORK AWARD

Awarded annually by the Canadian Authors Association to a Canadian author who has published at least four books inspirational to young people.

HOSTING AN AUTHOR/ILLUSTRATOR VISIT

After introducing your students to the talented authors and illustrators interviewed in this book, you may want to go one step further and invite one or two to visit your school. Following are some tips for planning that visit.

DON'T

Don't plan long sessions with each class. Unless your visitor has a special workshop prepared, forty-five minutes to an hour is about standard for a meet-the-author workshop.

Don't ask an author or illustrator to speak to more than thirty or forty students at a time, unless he has agreed in advance to address the entire student body. In fact, some may request even smaller groups, preferring intimate library readings and personal question-and-answer periods.

Don't expect your visitor to read or critique students' work, unless she has agreed to do so in advance. This is a time-consuming task and one that detracts from the author's visit. Remember, you've invited this person to come and talk about her work, not to mark papers.

Don't leave the room while your visitor is giving his presentation. Authors and illustrators are not teachers and cannot be expected to control or discipline your students when you are out of the room.

Don't abandon your visitor in the staff room. Let everyone know that an author or illustrator is visiting the school and make sure that she gets a cup of coffee on arrival and meets the rest of the staff.

Don't saddle your visitor with thank-you letters and pictures from every student in the class. Authors and illustrators on school visits carry enough paper already, without having to be loaded down with hundreds of letters that they simply don't have time to read or answer.

DO

Plan your visit as early as possible. Many authors and illustrators accept only a few invitations a year, reserving the rest of their time for work.

Make sure that someone is available to take care of your visitor at all times, and be sure to introduce him or her to the school principal and to the teachers whose classes will be participating in the workshops. Also, be sure to point out the staff room, washrooms, library, telephone, etc.

Provide your visitor with a typed schedule of planned events in advance, indicating how long each session will be and when breaks are planned.

Tell your visitor about special writing programs or other meet-the-author visits you've had at your school to help him prepare for your visit. Students who have met with and spoken to several authors will be a very different audience from those who have never explored the writing process in a workshop environment.

Be sure to have available any chart paper, dictionaries, projectors and tables that your visitor might need. At the very least, remind students to bring sharpened pencils and plenty of paper to the workshop. The more prepared students are, the more time can be devoted to working with the author or illustrator.

Try to have the workshop location available and empty at least fifteen minutes before the session begins. This will allow your presenter time to set things up for the workshops and collect her thoughts.

Make sure that you and your students have read at least one of the visiting author's books. It's also a good idea to prepare for the question-and-answer period in advance to avoid running out of meaningful questions. (How often have visiting authors and illustrators been confronted with the terrible three: How old are you? Where do you get your ideas? and How much money do you make?)

Have on display as many of your visitor's books as possible and provide students with the opportunity to browse through them before the author or illustrator arrives.

Be sure to pay attention while your visitor is giving his presentation. Although it may be tempting to mark those last few papers while you have the chance, guest speakers need your attention as much as that of your students. Otherwise, how will you be able to comment on their presentation during the break?

Give your visitor one thank-you note. He or she will have time to read and enjoy it and have space in the car to take it home. Or better yet, why not send a birthday card later in the year reminding that person how much you enjoyed their visit? We've listed the birthdays of the authors and illustrators included in this book on page 131, but you might even want to add them to your class calendar.

WHAT TO DO IF YOU CAN'T GET AN AUTHOR OR ILLUSTRATOR TO VISIT

Professional writers and illustrators don't just work for children's publishers. Try inviting newspaper or magazine authors, illustrators, book designers and editors to visit your school and talk about their work. Even if you have lined up a children's author it may still be worthwhile to invite one of these people to show students how different types of publications are produced.

You may also be able to make special arrangements to correspond on paper, via e-mail or through the magic of video with your favourite author or illustrator. This, of course, would really depend on the author or illustrator and would require a fair bit of planning at your end. Try to let the students do as much of the work as possible and do whatever you can to make things easy for your "writer in correspondence."

Students may also be fascinated to meet some of the people who work in a publishing house (editors, art directors, marketing representatives). You could also arrange for them to tour a printing press or book bindery, to see how the books are actually made, after they have been written and edited.

NEED HELP?

The Canadian Children's Book Centre has an extensive library of Canadian children's books, author/illustrator biographies and resource materials. They also sell author kits and publishing information packs for classrooms. Contact the centre for more information at:

> The Canadian Children's Book Centre
> 40 Orchard View Blvd.
> Toronto, Ontario M4R 1B9
> (416) 975-0010
> E-mail: ccbc@bookcentre.ca

The Storytellers' School of Toronto offers courses for budding storytellers; these are particularly helpful for librarians and teachers who enjoy reading aloud. Professional storytellers are also available for classroom visits. Call (416) 656-2445 for more information.

A call to a professional writers' organization is one of the best ways to book an author visit for your school:

> CANSCAIP (Canadian Society of Children's Authors, Illustrators and Performers)
> 40 Orchard View Blvd.
> Toronto, Ontario M4R 1B9
> Phone: (416) 515-1559
> Fax: (416) 515-7022

> The Writers' Union of Canada
> 40 Wellington Street East, Third Floor
> Toronto, Ontario M5E 1C7
> Phone: (416) 703-8982
> Fax: (416) 504-7656

> Canadian Authors Association
> 320 South Shores Road
> Campbellford, Ontario K0L 1L0
> Phone: (705) 653-0323

You might also try calling individual publishers to line up your meet-the-author workshop.

BIRTHDAYS

January 1	PHILIPPE BÉHA	August 1	MICHAEL MARTCHENKO
January 2	JEAN LITTLE	August 12	BRIAN DOYLE
January 12	KIM LAFAVE	August 12	CHRISTIANE DUCHESNE
January 14	CORA TAYLOR	August 12	TIM WYNNE-JONES
January 21	JULIE JOHNSTON	August 31	DENNIS LEE
February 10	BRENDA CLARK	August 31	KENNETH OPPEL
February 22	PAUL KROPP	September 1	BARBARA SMUCKER
March 3	ERIC WALTERS	September 4	KIM FERNANDES
March 11	NORAH MCCLINTOCK	September 12	KEVIN MAJOR
March 13	RUKHSANA KHAN	September 14	BARBARA GREENWOOD
March 29	MARGARET BUFFIE	September 25	EUGENIE FERNANDES
March 29	TED STAUNTON	October 20	JO ELLEN BOGART
March 31	IAN WALLACE	October 23	GORDON KORMAN
April 4	PHOEBE GILMAN	October 30	ROBIN MULLER
April 27	MICHAEL ARVAARLUK KUSUGAK	November 3	MONICA HUGHES
April 30	KIT PEARSON	November 3	BERNICE THURMAN HUNTER
May 3	MAXINE TROTTIER	November 9	JULIE LAWSON
May 19	SARAH ELLIS	November 14	CAROL MATAS
May 26	RON BRODA	November 16	BARBARA REID
May 29	MICHÈLE LEMIEUX	November 20	JANET WILSON
June 4	MARYANN KOVALSKI	November 20	WERNER ZIMMERMANN
June 11	ROBERT MUNSCH	November 22	LINDA GRANFIELD
June 17	MARIE-LOUISE GAY	November 24	ERIC WILSON
June 24	RON LIGHTBURN	November 28	SYLVIE DAIGNEAULT
June 25	TOLOWA MOLLEL	November 29	ERIC BEDDOWS
June 26	MICHAEL BEDARD	December 3	SHEREE FITCH
June 28	SHELLEY TANAKA	December 6	STÉPHANE POULIN
July 4	KAREN RECZUCH	December 13	KARLEEN BRADFORD
July 20	PAULETTE BOURGEOIS	December 21	CLAIRE MACKAY
July 22	KADY MACDONALD DENTON	December 28	JANET LUNN

ON BECOMING
A BETTER WRITER

When we asked the authors featured in this book how students become better writers, every one of them said, Read, read, read. We also asked what their favourite books were when they were kids, and some books came up several times. These included:

The 500 Hats of Bartholomew Cubbins by Dr. Seuss.
The Alpine Path by L.M. Montgomery.
Anne of Green Gables by L.M. Montgomery.
Angus Is Lost by Marjorie Flack.
The Babar books by Jean de Brunhoff.
The Borrowers by Mary Norton.
Charlotte's Web by E.B. White.
Emily of New Moon by L.M. Montgomery
Farmer Boy by Laura Ingalls Wilder.
Girl of the Limberlost by Gene Stratton-Porter.
The Great Brain series by John D. Fitzgerald.
The Hardy Boys series by Franklin W. Dixon.
Homer Price by Robert McCloskey.
Little House on the Prairie by Laura Ingalls Wilder.
Little Women by Louisa May Alcott.
The Nancy Drew series by Carolyn Keene.
The Ramona books by Beverly Cleary.
The Secret Garden by Frances Hodgson Burnett.
Stuart Little by E.B. White.
A Tree Grows in Brooklyn by Betty Smith.
The Wind in the Willows by Kenneth Grahame.
The Wizard of Oz by Frank L. Baum.
comic books
"Anything I could get my hands on!"

The writers also agreed on something else: they said, Write, write, write. The act of writing itself helps make you a better writer. Here are some idea starters for writing projects in your classroom:

The first rule of writing is to write about what you know. If you're the star player on the basketball team, write about that; if after school you help out with the family business, write

about that. You'll find that because you're a kind of an expert on the subject, you'll never run out of ideas. You could also write about something very personal, like your best moment ever.

When you just can't think of anything to write about, work with a partner and write each other a few great opening lines. Try not to include too much information in these sentences. The idea is to jumpstart your imagination, not block it with all kinds of facts that will have to be worked in later. Try something like "Twenty minutes into his detention, Bob heard something moving inside his desk." or "As soon as she saw the worms, she knew she was in trouble."

Another way of coming up with ideas is to make a list of "what ifs." What if we were snowed in and couldn't leave the school for a week? What if I stopped chewing on pencils and started eating them instead? After you've come up with at least twenty of these — the wilder, the better — pick your favourite and begin writing.

In a group, create a word-at-a-time story. (You'll need at least five people and a large piece of chart paper to do this one.) Begin by writing the words "once upon a time" at the top of the page, then each person in turn must add one word to the story. Continue taking turns until the story is finished.

A variation on the word-at-a-time story is a page-at-a-time story in which each person writes an entire page of the story before passing it on to the next person.

Try writing a favourite story from a different point of view. For instance, write the story of *Snow White* from the dwarves' point of view. Be careful to include only information that your new storyteller would know. You could also try writing a different ending for a favourite picture book or novel.

Draw a shape on a piece of paper, then on a separate sheet explain exactly how you drew it so someone else will be able to draw the same thing without looking at your picture. Then see how well your description worked. Is your writing precise?

Stretch your imagination by writing a tall tale to answer a simple question, such as, Where did you get those shoes? or, How long have you been waiting for the bus?

Mystery writers spend a great deal of time plotting out every detail of their stories. Plan the perfect crime for a mystery story of your own. (Remember, it's easiest if you write about what you know!)

Write a letter to the editor of a local newspaper or magazine. Or start your own school newsletter for kids who like the same things you do. For example, if you like sports, your newsletter could include game scores, your own thoughts on how certain teams are doing, and information on upcoming sports events in your school and in your town or city.

How good is your memory? Write a page or two describing everything you saw on your way to school today. Try to use as much detail as possible.

At one time, practically every school had a school song that described just what made their school special. Write a song about your school or class.

Write and illustrate your own picture book, then share it with a group of younger students in your school.

Rudyard Kipling's *Just So Stories* and the fables and legends of many aboriginal peoples provide explanations of how to the world came to be the way it is. Read some of these stories yourself, then write your own story to explain how the camel got his hump or why it snows in winter.

Suppose you were to become an author in ten years. Write a page about yourself for our 2012 edition of *Meet Canadian Authors and Illustrators*.

ON BECOMING A
BETTER ARTIST

It may surprise some readers to know that, just like the writers, practically every artist we talked to said the best way to become a better children's book illustrator is to read, read, read. That is, study the very best picture books by the very best illustrators for ideas and inspiration. Then study everything around you. Observe. Keep notes. Take photographs. Make sketches. Just like a writer collects ideas for new projects, so must an illustrator gather reference material.

As well, many of the artists interviewed talked about the importance of experimenting with different media and techniques until they found the ones that suited them best. There is no one correct way to illustrate for children's books. As you've seen from the books recommended in this collection, pretty much everything goes. Following are some of the media used by the many talented artists in this book: paper sculpture, Fimo, Plasticine, photography, watercolour, acrylic paints, oil paints, charcoal, pencils, gouache and collage.

Here are some idea starters for illustration projects in your classroom:

Try thinking in three dimensions. Paper sculptors and artists who work with modelling clay create three-dimensional pictures, which are then photographed for two-dimensional representation in a book.

Work from a different perspective. Instead of drawing every page face-on, try illustrating from a bird's-eye view, from below, from very close up or from very far away.

Use a picture as reference instead of working entirely from memory. Many illustrators first photograph their subject matter or look for existing pictures in books and library collections.

Practise drawing faces by looking at yourself in the mirror and drawing what you see.

Think about colour, texture and pattern. Instead of plain white paper, create your illustrations on wrapping paper, coloured construction paper, sandpaper or fabric. Or try rubbing a pencil or crayon on paper over a richly textured surface to create an unusual background for your work.

Combine several media to create a look that is uniquely your own. Why not try mixing paper sculpture and coloured pencils? Photography and collage? Clay and paint?

Look at ordinary things in a different way. Change and combine found objects to create illustrations with a twist. An apple with a hat and face? A toothbrush with wings? Follow your inspiration.

Artists begin their studies by drawing only in black and white. Try it yourself and see how it changes the way you look at things.

Your Classroom Publishing Centre

Following are some great books to help get
your gang going on their own publishing projects.

75 Creative Ways to Publish Students' Writing.
Copyright © 1999 by Cherlyn Sunflower.
Scholastic Inc.

350 Fabulous Writing Prompts. Copyright © 1999
by Jacqueline Sweeney. Scholastic Inc.

Author: A True Story. Copyright © 1997 by Helen
Lester. Houghton Mifflin Co.

The Big Book of Picture-Book Authors & Illustrators.
Copyright © 2001 by James Preller. Scholastic Inc.

Behind the Story. Copyright © 1995 by Barbara
Greenwood. Pembroke Publishers Ltd.

BOOK. Copyright © 1999 by George Ella Lyon.
Illustrated by Peter Catalanotto. DK Publishing.

A Caldecott Celebration. Copyright © 1998 by
Leonard S. Marcus. Walker & Co.

The CANSCAIP Companion. Copyright © 1991 by
CANSCAIP Ltd. Pembroke Publishers Ltd.

Children's Books and Their Creators. Copyright
© 1995. Edited by Anita Silvey. Houghton
Mifflin Co.

Easy Bookmaking. Copyright © 1996 by Natalie
Walsh. Scholastic Inc.

From Pictures to Words. Copyright © 1995 by Janet
Stevens. Thomas Allen & Son.

*From Reader to Writer: Teaching Writing Through
Classic Children's Books.* Copyright © 2000 by
Sarah Ellis. Groundwood Books.

How a Book Is Made. Copyright © 1986 by Aliki.
HarperCollins Canada Ltd.

*How to Capture Live Authors and Bring Them to
Your Schools.* Copyright © 1986 by David Melton.
Landmark Editions.

Making Books Across the Curriculum. Copyright ©
1999 by Natalie Walsh. Scholastic Inc.

Meet the Authors and Illustrators. Copyright ©
2000 by Deborah Kovacs and James Preller.
Scholastic Inc.

Multicultural Books to Make and Share. Copyright
© 1999 by Susan K. Gaylord. Scholastic Inc.

*Ready, Set, Write!: Creative Ideas to Get Kids
Writing.* Copyright © 1996 by Debra Kuzbik.
Peguis Publishers Ltd.

The Storymakers: Illustrating Children's Books.
Copyright © 1999 by the Canadian Children's
Book Centre. Pembroke Publishers Ltd.

The Storymakers: Writing Children's Books.
Copyright © 2000 by the Canadian Children's
Book Centre. Pembroke Publishers Ltd.

A Treasury of the Great Children's Book Illustrators.
Copyright © 1997 by Susan E. Meyer. Harry N.
Abrams.

The Ultimate Guide to Classroom Publishing.
Copyright © 1999 by Judy Green. Pembroke
Publishers Ltd.

What Do Authors Do? Copyright © 1997 by Eileen
Christelow. Houghton Mifflin Co.

What Do Illustrators Do? Copyright © 1999 by
Eileen Christelow. Houghton Mifflin Co.

*Wings of an Artist: Children's Book Illustrators Talk
About Their Art.* Copyright © 1999 by Julie
Cummins. Harry N. Abrams.

Write from the Start. Copyright © 2001 by Robin
Bright. Peguis Publishers Ltd.

*Write Now!: How to Turn Your Ideas into Great
Books.* Copyright © 1988, 1996 by Karleen
Bradford. Scholastic Canada Ltd.

Writing. Copyright © 1992 by Amanda Lewis.
Kids Can Press Ltd.

Writing Your Best Picture Book Ever. Copyright ©
1994 by Kathy Stinson. Pembroke Publishers Ltd.

The Young Writer's Companion. Copyright © 1999
by Sarah Ellis. Groundwood Books.

ADDITIONAL RESOURCE MATERIALS

These two books are a great starting point for further research
into Canadian children's authors and illustrators:

The Storymakers: Illustrating Children's Books. © 1999 by The Canadian Children's Book Centre.
The Storymakers: Writing Children's Books. © 2000 by The Canadian Children's Book Centre.
Both published by Pembroke Publishers Ltd.

For links to individual author and illustrator Web sites, please visit: www.scholastic.ca

MICHAEL BEDARD

The Canadian Children's Book Centre. "Meet the Author: Michael Bedard." *Children's Book News*, Summer 1988.

"Michael Bedard." *Children's Literature Review*, Vol. 35.

Davis, Marie C. "An Interview with Michael Bedard." *Canadian Children's Literature*, No. 82, 1996.

Findon, Joanne. "Night Vision." *Quill & Quire*, April 1994.

Findon, Joanne. "Darkness in the Novels of Michael Bedard." *Canadian Children's Literature*, No. 82, 1996.

Greenwood, Barbara. "Picture Books Aren't Just for Preschoolers Anymore." *City Parent*, November 1997.

Steven, Laurence. "Excellent Alchemy" *Canadian Children's Literature*, No. 63, 1991.

ERIC BEDDOWS

The Canadian Children's Book Centre. "Introducing: Ken Nutt (Eric Beddows)." *Children's Book News*, Summer 1986.

The Canadian Children's Book Centre. "Profile." *Children's Book News*, Summer 1988.

Granfield, Linda. "The Art of the Children's Book Illustrator." *Quill & Quire*, October 1985.

Granfield, Linda. "Beyond the Shadows: The Illustrations of Eric Beddows." *Teaching Librarian*, Fall 1995.

Jenkinson, David. "Portraits: Eric Beddows, Award Winning Children's Illustrator." *Emergency Librarian*, May/June 1993.

Oppel, Kenneth. "Ken Nutt (a.k.a. Eric Beddows): Zooming to the Top." *Quill & Quire*, August 1989.

PHILIPPE BÉHA

Goedhart, Bernie. "Philippe Béha." *Quill & Quire*, October 1985.

JO ELLEN BOGART

Anderson, Rosemary. "Suddenly — Success for Guelph Writer." *The Daily Mercury*, February 25, 1988.

The Canadian Children's Book Centre. "Introducing: Jo Ellen Bogart." 1990.

Granfield, Linda. "Of Tropical Jungles and Runaway Soap." *Books in Canada*, December 1988.

Stinson, Kathy. "Introducing Jo Ellen Bogart." *CANSCAIP News*, Spring 1999.

PAULETTE BOURGEOIS

The Canadian Children's Book Centre. "Meet the Author: Paulette Bourgeois." *Children's Book News*, April 1987.

Renzetti, Elizabeth. "Franklin's Big Adventure in Corporateland." *Globe and Mail*, August 27, 1998.

Sheldrick Ross, Catherine. "An Interview with Paulette Bourgeois." *Canadian Children's Literature*, No. 49, 1988.

Wagner, Dale. "Introducing Paulette Bourgeois." *CANSCAIP News*, Winter 1992.

Turbide, Diane. "The KidLit Boom." *Maclean's*, December 11, 1995.

KARLEEN BRADFORD

Bradford, Karleen. Acceptance Speech for Canadian Library Association Young Adult Book Award. *Canadian Materials*, September 1993.

The Canadian Children's Book Centre. "Introducing: Karleen Bradford." 1989.

Kennedy, Janice. "Novelist Makes History Come Alive for Her Young Readers." *Ottawa Citizen*, January 18, 1993.

Gilmore, Anne. "Peripatetic Karleen Bradford Weaves Travels into YA Fiction." *Quill & Quire*, August 1985.

Garvie, Maureen. "Nomad Scribe." *Quill & Quire*, August 1986.

RON BRODA

3-D Paper Crafts. Copyright © 1997 by Ron Broda and Joanne Webb. Scholastic Canada Ltd.

MARGARET BUFFIE

Buffie, Margaret. "Back on This Side of the Door." *School Libraries in Canada*, Spring 1991.

The Canadian Children's Book Centre. "Introducing: Marget Buffie." 1990.

The Canadian Children's Book Centre. "Meet the Author: Marget Buffie." *Children's Book News*, Fall 1988.

Carver, Peter. "Margaret Buffie's Spirit Circle." *Quill & Quire*, November 1989.

Norrie, Helen. "Buffie Keeps Getting Better." *Winnipeg Free Press*, November 7, 1992.

Stinson, Kathy. "Introducing Margaret Buffie." *CANSCAIP News*, Fall 1994.

BRENDA CLARK

The Canadian Children's Book Centre. "Introducing: Brenda Clark." 1986.

Renzetti, Elizabeth. "Franklin's Big Adventure in Corporateland." *Globe and Mail*, August 27, 1998.

KADY MACDONALD DENTON

Alexander, Wilma. "Introducing Kady MacDonald Denton." *CANSCAIP News*, Winter 1991.

The Canadian Children's Book Centre. "Introducing: Kady MacDonald Denton." 1990.

Goldsmith, Annette. "Denton's Dictum: Paint Like a Child." *Quill & Quire*, February 1990.

Jenkinson, Dave. "Portraits: Kady MacDonald Denton, Watercolorist Extraordinaire." *Emergency Librarian*, May/June 1994.

Kusch, Larry. "Brandon Artist Produces Children's Books." *Brandon Sun*, September 7, 1988.

BRIAN DOYLE

Finlayson, Jane. "Brian Doyle Reveals 'Kid Inside Me.'" *Ottawa Citizen*, November 4, 1982.

Garvie, Maureen. "Up Doyle Way." *Quill & Quire*, March 1995.

Hedblad, Alan, ed. "Doyle, Brian 1935– ." *Something About the Author*. Gale Group, 1979. Vol. 16.

Kirchhoff, H.J. "Life on Easy Street." *Globe and Mail*, April 14, 1992.

Krumins, Anita. "Up When One Hung Low." *WQ Reviews*, 1983. Vol. 5.

MacCallum, Elizabeth. "Making Issues Meaningful Isn't Just Kid's Stuff." *Globe and Mail*, October 17, 1992.

Twigg, Alan. "According to Father Doyle." *The Magazine*, May 4, 1980.

SARAH ELLIS

Buchanan, Joan. "Introducing Sarah Ellis." *CANSCAIP News*, 1993.

Burns, John. "Profile: Sarah Ellis." *Children's Book News*, Winter 1987.

The Canadian Children's Book Centre. "Introducing: Sarah Ellis." 1990.

Jenkinson, Dave. "Profiles: Sarah Ellis." *Connecting Classrooms, Libraries & Canadian Learning Resources*, February 1997.

Kent, Jennifer McGrath. "An Interview with Sarah Ellis." *Canadian Children's Literature*, No. 89, 1998.

Saltman, Judith. "An Appreciation of Sarah Ellis." *Canadian Children's Literature*, 1992. Vol. 67.

"Sarah Ellis." *Children's Literature Review*, Vol. 42.

KIM FERNANDES

Jordan, Betty Ann. "Illustration's New Wave." *Quill & Quire*, February 1997.

McKay, Shona. "Meet the Author." *Imperial Oil Review*, Autumn 2001.

SHEREE FITCH

Babinski, Bob. "Storyteller Trips the Light Fantastic and Kids Love It." *Globe and Mail*, September 8, 1990.

Biehn, Janice. "Chere Sheree." *Chatelaine*, January 1996.

The Canadian Children's Book Centre. "Introducing: Sheree Fitch." 1990.

Faulder, Liane. "Author Pens Fun Nonsense." *Edmonton Journal*, May 16, 1995.

Jenkinson, Dave. "Portraits: Sheree Fitch." *Emergency Librarian*, September/October 1993.

MARIE-LOUISE GAY

Davis, Marie. "Un penchant pour la diagonale: An Interview with Marie-Louise Gay." *Canadian Children's Literature*, No. 60, 1990.

Greenwood, Barbara. "Moonbeam on a Cat's Ear and Rainy Day Magic: Questions and Answers with Marie-Louise Gay." *CANSCAIP News*, Winter 1986.

O'Brian, Leacy. "An Interview with Marie-Louise Gay." *Canadian Materials*, March 1989.

Olendorf, Donna, ed. "Gay, Marie-Louise 1952– ." *Something About the Author*. Gale Group, 1992. Vol. 68.

PHOEBE GILMAN

Commire, Anne, ed. "Gilman, Phoebe 1940– ."
Something About the Author. Gale Group, 1990.
Vol. 58.

Gaitskell, Susan. "Introducing Phoebe Gilman."
CANSCAIP News, Spring 1986.

O'Reilly, Gillian. "Phoebe Gilman: Winner of the 1993
Ruth Schwartz Award." *Canadian Bookseller*,
June/July 1993.

LINDA GRANFIELD

The Canadian Children's Book Centre. "Introducing:
Linda Granfield." 1990.

Brown, Louise. "Lively Book Teaches Kids About
Voting." *Toronto Star*, September 6, 1990.

Muldoon, Kathy. "A Circus Comes." *Toronto Star*,
October 18, 1997.

Wishinsky, Frieda. "Breathing History." *Books in
Canada*, February 1997.

Hedblad, Alan, ed. "Granfield, Linda 1950– ."
Something About the Author. Gale Group, 1998.
Vol. 96.

BERNICE THURMAN HUNTER

The Canadian Children's Book Centre. "Meet the
Author: Bernice Thurman Hunter." *Children's Book
News*, December 1983.

Commire, Anne, ed. "Hunter, Bernice Thurman
1922– ." *Something About the Author*. Gale Group,
1986. Vol. 45.

Evasuk, Stasia. "Age of Reason." *Toronto Star*,
September 9, 1982.

Greenwood, Barbara. "Introducing Bernice Thurman
Hunter." *CANSCAIP News*, Spring 1989.

Landsberg, Michele. "Book Takes Magic Look at
Toronto's Depression Era." *Toronto Star*, October 15,
1981.

Wilkins, Charles. "Bernice Thurman Hunter: A World
of Wonder from her Own Past." *Quill & Quire*,
October 1987.

MONICA HUGHES

Commire, Anne, ed. "Hughes, Monica 1925– ."
Something About the Author. Gale Group, 1979.
Vol. 15.

Greenwood, Barbara. "Introducing Monica Hughes."
CANSCAIP News, Spring 1984.

Hughes, Monica. "The Writer's Quest." *Canadian
Children's Literature*, No. 26, 1989.

Jones, Raymond E. "The Technological Pastoralist:
A Conversation with Monica Hughes." *Canadian
Children's Literature*, No. 44, 1988.

Malconnsen, Joan. "Writing Classics for Canadian Kids:
Monica Hughes." *Quill & Quire*, February 1980.

Nakamura, Joyce, ed. "Hughes, Monica, 1925– ."
Something About the Author Autobiography Series. Gale
Group, 1991. Vol. 11.

O'Reilly, Gillian. "Monica Hughes." *Jam Magazine*,
June 1984.

Olendorf, Donna and Diane Telgen, ed. "Hughes,
Monica (Ince), 1925-." *Something About the Author*.
Gale Group, 1993. Vol. 70.

Wishinsky, Frieda. "Monica Hughes: Master of Myth."
Quill & Quire, December 1989.

JULIE JOHNSTON

Ellis, Sarah. "News from the North." *The Horn Book
Magazine*, September-October 1994. Vol. LXX. No. 5.

Hedblad, Alan, ed. "Johnston, Julie– ." *Something About
the Author*. Gale Group, 1994. No. 78.

Peacock, Scot, ed. "Johnston, Julie." *Contemporary
Authors*. Gale Group, 1995.

Taylor, Bill. "Mint Julie." *Toronto Star*, December 22,
1992.

RUKHSANA KHAN

Jenkinson, Dave. "CM Profiles: Rukhsana Khan."
CM Magazine, 1999.

GORDON KORMAN

Commire, Anne, ed. "Korman, Gordon 1963– ."
Something About the Author. Gale Group, 1987.
Vol. 49.

Ferns, Chris. "An Interview with Gordon Korman."
Canadian Children's Literature, No. 38, 1985.

Morgan, Joanna. "Kid Lit." *Today Magazine*, June 6, 1981.

MARYANN KOVALSKI

Bildfell, Laurie. "The Art of the Children's Book
Illustrator." *Quill & Quire*, October 1985.

Commire, Anne, ed. "Kovalski, Maryann 1951– ."
Something About the Author. Gale Group, 1990.
Vol. 58.

Wagner, Dale. "Introducing Maryann Kovalski."
CANSCAIP News, Summer 1989.

PAUL KROPP

Commire, Ann, ed. "Kropp, Paul (Stephan) 1948– ."
Something About the Author. Gale Group, 1984.
Vol. 38.

Hancock, Pat. "Introducing Paul Kropp." *CANSCAIP
News*, Spring 1993.

Vanderhoof, Ann. "Hot Topics for Cool Readers." *Quill
& Quire*, January 1980.

DENNIS LEE

Commire, Anne, ed. "Lee, Dennis (Beynon) 1939– ."
Something About the Author. Gale Group, 1978. Vol. 14.

Lee, Dennis. "Roots and Play: Writing as a 35-Year-Old Children." *Canadian Children's Literature*, No. 4, 1976.

Ross, Catherine and Cory Bieman Davies. "Re-realizing Mother Goose: An Interview with Dennis Lee on Jelly Belly." *Canadian Children's Literature*, No. 33, 1984.

JEAN LITTLE

"An Interview with Jean Little." *Grail: An Ecumenical Journal*, December 1989.

Frazer, Frances. "Something on Jean Little." *Canadian Children's Literature*, No. 53, 1989.

Little by Little: A Writer's Education. Copyright © 1987 by Jean Little. Penguin Books Canada Ltd.

Nakamura, Joyce, ed. "Little, Jean 1932– ." *Something About the Author Autobiography Series*. Gale Group, 1989. Vol. 17.

Olendorf, Donna, ed. "Little, Jean 1932– ." *Something About the Author*. Gale Group, 1992. Vol. 68.

Ross, Catherine. "An Interview with Jean Little." *Canadian Children's Literature*, No. 34, 1984.

Stars Come Out Within. Copyright © 1990 by Jean Little. Penguin Books Canada Ltd.

JANET LUNN

Barkhouse, Joyce. "Introducing Janet Lunn." *CANSCAIP News*, Spring 1985.

Nakamura, Joyce, ed. "Lunn, Janet 1928– ." *Something About the Author Autobiography Series*. Gale Group, 1991. Vol. 12.

Olendorf, Donna, ed. "Lunn, Janet 1928– ." *Something About the Author*. Gale Group, 1992. Vol. 68.

CLAIRE MACKAY

Commire, Anne, ed. "Mackay, Claire 1930– ." *Something About the Author*. Gale Group, 1985. Vol. 40.

Mackay, Claire. "Real Plums in Imaginary Cakes." *Canadian Children's Literature*, No. 54, 1989.

KEVIN MAJOR

Commire, Ann, ed. "Major, Kevin 1949– ." *Something About the Author*. Gale Group, 1983. Vol. 32.

"Kevin Major 1949– ." *Children's Literature Review*, Vol. 11

Posesorski, Sherie. "Kevin Major." *Books in Canada*, December 1984.

"Tales of Newfoundland Youth Spell Success for Kevin Major." *Atlantic Insight*, November 1984.

MICHAEL MARTCHENKO

Commire, Anne, ed. "Martchenko, Michael 1942– ." *Something About the Author*. Gale Group, 1988. Vol. 50.

Vanderhoof, Ann. "The Art of the Children's Book Illustrator." *Quill & Quire*, October 1985.

NORAH MCCLINTOCK

Barclay, Pat. "Live and Learn." *Books in Canada*, November 1992.

Jenkinson, Dave. "Portraits: Norah McClintock." *Emergency Librarian*, March/April 1993.

TOLOLWA MOLLEL

Greenwood, Barbara. "Introducing Tololwa M. Mollel." *CANSCAIP News*, Spring 1992.

Huser, Glen. "African Tales Best Read Aloud." *Edmonton Journal*, January 18, 1998.

Jenkinson, Dave. "Portraits: Tololwa M. Mollel." *Emergency Librarian*, January/February 1994.

Van Luven, Lynne. "Feasting With Words." *Edmonton Journal*, August 1990.

ROBIN MULLER

The Canadian Children's Book Centre. "Meet the Author: Robin Muller." *Children's Book News*, March 1985.

Greenwood, Barbara. "Introducing Robin Muller." *CANSCAIP News*, Spring 1990.

ROBERT MUNSCH

The Canadian Children's Book Centre. "Meet the Author: Robert Munsch." *Book Times*, September 1981.

Collins, Janet. "Giant Problem or What Is a Kid's Book Anyway?" *Canadian Materials*, May 1990.

Commire, Anne, ed. "Munsch, Robert N. 1945– ." *Something About the Author*. Gale Group, 1988. Vol. 50.

Crawford, C. Lee. "Happy Anniversary, Bob!" *Quill & Quire*, April 1989.

Kondo, David. "Robert Munsch: An Interview." *Canadian Children's Literature*, No. 43, 1986.

Williamson, Barb. "Lunch with Munsch." *Edmonton Journal*, March 8, 2001.

KENNETH OPPEL

Bethune, Brian. "High-flying Tales for Tweens." *Maclean's*, November 22, 1999.

Ellis, Sarah. "Sunwing Soars." *Quill & Quire*, August 1999.

Jenkinson, Dave. "Portraits: Kenneth Oppel." *Emergency Librarian*, May/June 1997.

Ross, Val. "Bat Books Have Taken Wing." *Globe and Mail*, September 17, 1999.

KIT PEARSON
Schwartz, Ellen. "Introducing Kit Pearson." *CANSCAIP News*, Summer 1990.

STÉPHANE POULIN
Goedhart, Bernie. "Stéphane Poulin's Sensitive Approach to Life and Art." *Quill & Quire*, August 1987.

KAREN RECZUCH
Reczuch, Karen. "Amelia Frances Howard-Gibbon Award — Karen Reczuch." *Feliciter*, July/August 1991.
Reczuch, Karen. "Struggling with Success: An Illustrator Confesses." *Children's Book News*. Summer/Fall 1997.

BARBARA REID
The Canadian Children's Book Centre. "Meet the Illustrator: Barbara Reid." *Children's Book News*, September 1985.
Graitskell, Susan. "An Interview with Barbara Reid." *Canadian Children's Literature*, No. 56, 1989.
McDougall, Carol. "Introducing Barbara Reid." *CANSCAIP News*, Spring 1988.

BARBARA SMUCKER
"Barbara (Claassen) Smucker 1915– " *Children's Literature Review*, Vol. 10.
The Canadian Children's Book Centre. "Meet the Author: Barbara Smucker." *Book Times*, 1980.
Davies, Cory Bieman. "An Interview with Barbara Smucker." *Canadian Children's Literature*, No. 22, 1981.
Nakamura, Joyce, ed. "Barbara (Claassen) Smucker 1915– ." *Something About the Author Autobiography Series*. Gale Group, 1991. Vol. 11.
Salata, Estelle. "Barbara Smucker." *CANSCAIP News*, Fall 1990.

TED STAUNTON
The Canadian Children's Book Centre. "Meet the Author: Ted Staunton." *Children's Book News*, June 1985.

SHELLEY TANAKA
Barrett, Sylvia. "Tanaka's Pastoral Idyll." *Quill & Quire*, October 1991.
O'Reilly, Gillian. "The Two Hats (and Many Books) of Shelley Tanaka." *Children's Book News*, Spring 1999.

MAXINE TROTTIER
Trottier, Maxine. "Book of the Year for Children Award." *Feliciter*, July/August 1996.

IAN WALLACE
The Canadian Children's Book Centre. "Meet the Author: Ian Wallace." *Children's Book News*, June 1984.
Commire, Anne, ed. "Wallace, Ian 1950– ." *Something About the Author*. Gale Group, 1989. Vol. 56.
Wallace, Ian. "When Fort Nelson's Kids Won Ian Wallace." *Quill & Quire*, February 1985.

ERIC WALTERS
Oppel, Kenneth. "Walters Has a Tiger By the Tail." *Quill & Quire*, April 1999.

ERIC WILSON
Commire, Ann, ed. "Wilson, Eric H. 1940– ." *Something About the Author*. Gale Group, 1984. Vol. 34.
Eric Wilson's Canada. (video) Magic Lantern Communications, 1991.
Jenkinson, Dave. "Eric Wilson." *Profiles 2*, The Canadian Library Association, 1982.
Locher, Frances C., ed. "Wilson, Eric H." *Contemporary Authors*, Gale Group, 1981.
Meet the Author: Eric Wilson. (film strip and video) School Services of Canada, 1987. Senn, Roma.
"Whodunit? Eric Wilson." *Atlantic Insight*, October 1981.

TIM WYNNE-JONES
The Canadian Children's Book Centre. "Introducing: Tim Wynne-Jones." 1986.
Fogel, Melanie. "Tim Wynne-Jones." *Canadian Materials*, November 1988.
McPhee, Joyce. "Profile: Tim Wynne-Jones." *Canadian Materials*, January 1994.
Manguel, Alberto. "The Storyteller." *Toronto Life*, November 1984.
Oughton, John. "Edifice Complex." *Books in Canada*, December 1986.
Wynne-Jones, Tim. "Chasing a Piano Suspended in the Sky." *Feliciter*, July/August 1996.

WERNER ZIMMERMANN
Maruszeczka, Greg. "Being There." *Canadian Materials*, September 1993.
O'Brien, Leacy. "Watermelon Blue." *Canadian Materials*, May 1990.

PHOTOGRAPHY CREDITS

Author/illustrator photographs

Michael Bedard © Merilee Brand; Brian Doyle © John Bladen Bentley; Christiane Duchesne © Martine Doyon, courtesy of Les éditions du boréale; Sheree Fitch © Noel Chenier; Phoebe Gilman © Brian Bender; Linda Granfield © Dan Callis; Julie Johnston courtesy of Stoddart Kids; Michael Kusugak courtesy of Annick Press; Julie Lawson © Patrick Lawson; Dennis Lee courtesy of Key Porter Books; Michèle Lemieux courtesy of Kids Can Press; Ron Lightburn © Dave Hines; Carol Matas © Thomas Fricke; Tololwa Mollel © The Edmonton Arts Council; Kit Pearson courtesy of Penguin Books Canada; Stéphane Poulin courtesy of Les 400 coups; Karen Reczuch © Craig Hyde Parker; Barbara Reid © Ian Crysler; Barbara Smucker © de Vries Studio, courtesy of Stoddart Kids; Ted Staunton courtesy of Red Deer Press; Shelley Tanaka © Gill Foss; Cora Taylor © Benje Bondar; Tim Wynne-Jones courtesy of Groundwood Books; Werner Zimmermann © Koster Photography, courtesy of Stoddart Kids.

Book covers

MICHAEL BEDARD
Emily © 1992 by Michael Bedard. Illustrations © 1992 by Barbara Cooney. Reprinted by permission of Random House Children's Books, a division of Random House, Inc.; *Redwork* © 1992 by Michael Bedard. Cover illustration by Laura Fernandez and Rick Jacobson. Reprinted by permission of Stoddart Kids.

ERIC BEDDOWS
Circus © 1997 by Linda Granfield. Cover illustration © 1997 by Eric Beddows. Reprinted by permission of Groundwood Books/Douglas & McIntyre Ltd.; *Night Cars* © 1988 by Teddy Jam. Illustrations © 1988 by Eric Beddows. Reprinted by permission of Groundwood Books/Douglas & McIntyre Ltd.

PHILIPPE BÉHA
Biscuits in the Cupboard © 1997 by Barbara Nichol . Illustrations © 1997 by Philippe Béha. Reprinted by permission of Stoddart Kids; *What Do the Fairies Do With All Those Teeth?* © 1991 by Michel Luppens. Illustrations © 1989 by Philippe Béha. Reprinted by permission of Scholastic Canada Ltd.

JO ELLEN BOGART
Jeremiah Learns to Read © 1999 by Jo Ellen Bogart. Illustrations © 1999 by Laura Fernandes and Rick Jacobson. Reprinted by permission of Scholastic Canada Ltd.; *The Night the Stars Flew* © 2001 by Jo Ellen Bogart. Illustrations © 2001 by Ginette Beaulieu. Reprinted by permission of Scholastic Canada Ltd.

PAULETTE BOURGEOIS
Oma's Quilt © 2001 by Paulette Bourgeois. Illustrations © 2001 by Stephane Jorisch. Reprinted by permission of Kids Can Press Ltd.; *The Moon* © 1997 by Paulette Bourgeois. Illustrations © 1997 by Bill Slavin. Reprinted by permission of Kids Can Press Ltd.

KARLEEN BRADFORD
Dragonfire © 1997 by Karleen Bradford. Reprinted by permission of HarperCollins Publishers Ltd.; *Whisperings of Magic* © 2001 by Karleen Bradford. Reprinted by permission of HarperCollins Publishers Ltd.

RON BRODA
Dinosaur: Digging Up a Giant © 1999 by Chris McGowan. Illustrations © 1999 by Ron Broda. Reprinted by permission of Scholastic Canada Ltd.; *Have You Seen Bugs?* © 1996 by Joanne Oppenheim. Illustrations © 1996 by Ron Broda. Reprinted by permission of Scholastic Canada Ltd.

MARGARET BUFFIE
Angels Turn Their Backs © 1988 by Margaret Buffie. Cover illustration by Florentina Bogdan. Reprinted by permission of Kids Can Press Ltd.; *The Watcher* © 2000 by Margaret Buffie. Cover illustration by Marie Bartholomew. Reprinted by permission of Kids Can Press Ltd.

BRENDA CLARK
Franklin and Harriet © 2001 by Paulette Bourgeois. Illustrations © 2001 by Brenda Clark. Reprinted by permission of Kids Can Press Ltd.; *Sadie and the Snowman* © 1985 by Allen Morgan. Illustrations © 1985 by Brenda Clark. Reprinted by permission of Kids Can Press Ltd.

SYLVIE DAIGNEAULT
Bruno Falls Asleep © 2000 by Sylvie Daigneault. Reprinted by permission of HarperCollins Publishers Ltd.; *All on a Sleepy Night* © 2001 by Shutta Crum. Illustrations © 2001 by Sylvie Daigneault. Reprinted by permission of Stoddart Kids.

KADY MACDONALD DENTON
A Child's Treasury of Nursery Rhymes © 1998 by Kady MacDonald Denton. Reprinted by permission of Kids Can Press Ltd.; *I Wished for a Unicorn* © 2000 by Robert Heidbreder. Illustrations © 2000 by Kady MacDonald Denton. Reprinted by permission of Kids Can Press Ltd.

BRIAN DOYLE
Mary Ann Alice © 2001 by Brian Doyle. Reprinted by permission of Groundwood Books/Douglas & McIntyre Ltd.; *Uncle Ronald* © 1995 by Brian Doyle. Reprinted by permission of Groundwood Books/Douglas & McIntyre Ltd.

JULIE LAWSON
Goldstone © 1997 by Julie Lawson. Cover illustration by Ken Campbell. Reprinted by permission of Stoddart Kids; *Emma and the Silk Train* © 1997 by Julie Lawson. Illustrations © 1997 by Paul Mombourquette. Reprinted by permission of Kids Can Press Ltd.

DENNIS LEE
Bubblegum Delicious © 2000 by Dennis Lee. Illustrations © 2000 by David McPhail. Reprinted by permission of Key Porter Books Ltd.; *The Ice Cream Store* © 1991 by Dennis Lee. Illustrations by David McPhail. Reprinted by permission of HarperCollins Canada Ltd.

MICHÈLE LEMIEUX
Stormy Night © 1999 by Michèle Lemieux. Reprinted by permission of Kids Can Press Ltd.; *There Was an Old Man* © 1984 by Edward Lear. Illustrations by Michèle Lemieux. Reprinted by permission of Kids Can Press Ltd.

RON LIGHTBURN
Driftwood Cove © 1998 by Sandra Lightburn. Illustrations © 1998 by Ron Lightburn. Reprinted by permission of Doubleday Canada, a division of Random House of Canada Ltd.; *Wild Girl and Gran* © 2000 by Nan Gregory. Illustrations © 2000 by Ron Lightburn. Reprinted by permission of Red Deer Press.

JEAN LITTLE
Orphan at My Door © 2001 by Jean Little. Reprinted by permission of Scholastic Canada Ltd.; *Willow and Twig* © 2000 by Jean Little. Reprinted by permission of Penguin Books Canada Ltd.

JANET LUNN
The Hollow Tree © 1997 by Janet Lunn. Reprinted by permission of Alfred A. Knopf Canada, a division of Random House of Canada Ltd.; *The Story of Canada* © 2000 by Janet Lunn. Reprinted by permission of Key Porter Books Ltd.

CLAIRE MACKAY
First Folks and Vile Voyageurs © 2001 by Claire Mackay. Cover illustration by Bill Dickson. Reprinted by permission of Scholastic Canada Ltd.; *Laughs* © 1997 by Claire Mackay. Cover illustration by Loris Lesynski. Reprinted by permission of Tundra Books.

KEVIN MAJOR
Eh? to Zed © 2000 by Kevin Major. Illustrations © 2000 by Alan Daniel. Reprinted by permission of Red Deer Press; *The House of Wooden Santas* © 1997 by Kevin Major. Woodcarvings by Imelda George. Photography by Ned Pratt. Reprinted by permission of Red Deer Press.

MICHAEL MARTCHENKO
Matthew and the Midnight Bank © 2000 by Allen Morgan. Illustrations by Michael Martchenko. Reprinted by permission of Stoddart Kids; *Up, Up, Down* © 2001 by Robert Munsch. Illustrations by Michael Martchenko. Reprinted by permission of Scholastic Canada Ltd.

CAROL MATAS
Cloning Miranda © 1999 by Carol Matas. Reprinted by permission of Scholastic Canada Ltd.; *Daniel's Story* © 1993 by Carol Matas. Reprinted by permission of Scholastic Inc.

NORAH MCCLINTOCK
The Body in the Basement © 1997 by Norah McClintock. Reprinted by permission of Scholastic Canada Ltd.; *Over the Edge* © 2000 by Norah McClintock. Reprinted by permission of Scholastic Canada Ltd.

TOLOLWA MOLLEL
Subira, Subira © 2000 by Tololwa Mollel. Illustrations © 2000 by Laura Saport. Reprinted by permission of Clarion Books/Houghton Mifflin; *To Dinner, for Dinner* © 2000 by Tololwa Mollel. Illustrations © 2000 by Synthia Saint James. Reprinted by permission of Holiday House.

ROBIN MULLER
Badger's New House © 2002 by Robin Muller. Reprinted by permission of Scholastic Canada Ltd.; *The Happy Prince* by Oscar Wilde. Illustrations © 2001 by Robin Muller. Reprinted by permission of Stoddart Kids.

ROBERT MUNSCH
Love You Forever © 1986 by Bob Munsch Enterprises. Illustrations © 1986 by Sheila McGraw. Reprinted by permission of Firefly Books; *Alligator Baby* © 1997 by Bob Munsch Enterprises. Illustrations © 1997 by Michael Martchenko. Reprinted by permission of Scholastic Canada Ltd.

KENNETH OPPEL
Silverwing © 1997 by Kenneth Oppel. Reprinted by permission of HarperCollins Publishers Ltd.; *Sunwing* © 1999 by Kenneth Oppel. Reprinted by permission of HarperCollins Publishers Ltd.

KIT PEARSON
Awake and Dreaming © 1996 by Kit Pearson. Reprinted by permission of Penguin Books Canada Ltd.; *The Sky is Falling* © 1989 by Kit Pearson. Reprinted by permission of Penguin Books Canada Ltd.

STÉPHANE POULIN
Old Thomas and the Little Fairy © 2000 by Dominique Demers. Illustrations © 2000 by Stéphane Poulin. Reprinted by permission of Dominique & Friends; *Can You Catch Josephine?* © 1937 by Stéphane Poulin. Reprinted by permission of Tundra Books.

KAREN RECZUCH
The Ghost Cat © 2001 by Mark Abley. Illustrations by Karen Reczuch. Reprinted by permission of Groundwood Books/Douglas & McIntyre Ltd.; *Just Like New* © 1995 by Ainslie Manson. Illustrations by Karen Reczuch. Reprinted by permission of Groundwood Books/Douglas & McIntyre Ltd.

BAREARA REID
The Golden Goose © 2000 by Barbara Reid. Reprinted by permission of Scholastic Canada Ltd.; *The Party* © 1997 by Barbara Reid. Reprinted by permission of Scholastic Canada Ltd.

BARBARA SMUCKER
Underground to Canada © 1977 by Barbara Smucker. Reprinted by permission of Penguin Books Canada Ltd.; *Selina and the Shoo-Fly Pie* © 1995 by Barbara Smucker. Illustrations © 1995 by Janet Wilson. Reprinted by permission of Stoddart Kids.

TED STAUNTON
Hope Springs a Leak © 1998 by Ted Staunton. Reprinted by permission of Red Deer Press; *Puddleman* © 1999 by Ted Staunton. Illustrations © 1999 by Brenda Clark. Reprinted by permission of Red Deer Press.

SHELLEY TANAKA
Footnotes: Dancing the World's Best Loved Ballets © 2001 by Frank Augustyn and Shelley Tanaka. Reprinted by permission of Key Porter Books Ltd.; *In the Time of Knights* © 2001 by The Madison Press Limited. Written by Shelley Tanaka. Illustrations by Greg Ruhl. Reprinted by permission of Madison Press.

CORA TAYLOR
Julie's Secret © 1991 by Cora Taylor. Reprinted by permission of Groundwood Books/Douglas & McIntyre Ltd.; *On Wings of a Dragon* © 2001 by Cora Taylor. Reprinted by permission of Fitzhenry & Whiteside.

MAXINE TROTTIER
A Circle of Silver © 1999 by Maxine Trottier. Cover illustration by Al Van Mil. Reprinted by permission of Stoddart Kids; *Claire's Gift* © 1999 by Maxine Trottier. Illustrations by Rajka Kupesic. Reprinted by permission of Scholastic Canada Ltd.

IAN WALLACE
Boy of the Deeps © 1998 by Ian Wallace. Reprinted by permission of Groundwood Books/Douglas & McIntyre Ltd.; *The Name of the Tree* © 1989 by Celia Barker Lottridge. Illustrations © 1989 by Ian Wallace. Reprinted by permission of Groundwood Books/Douglas & McIntyre Ltd..

ERIC WALTERS
The Bully Boys © 2000 by Eric Walters. Reprinted by permission of Penguin Books Canada Ltd.; *Rebound* © 2000 by Eric Walters. Cover illustration by Sharif Tarabay. Reprinted by permission of Stoddart Kids.

ERIC WILSON
Code Red at the Supermall © 1988 by Eric Wilson. Reprinted by permission of HarperCollins Publishers Ltd.; *Murder on the Canadian* © 1983 by Eric Wilson. Reprinted by permission of HarperCollins Publishers Ltd.

JANET WILSON
In Flanders Fields © 1999 by Linda Granfield. Illustrations © 1999 by Janet Wilson. Reprinted by permission of Stoddart Kids; *Selina and the Bear Paw Quilt* © 1998 by Barbara Smucker. Illustrations © 1998 by Janet Wilson. Reprinted by permission of Stoddart Kids.

TIM WYNNE-JONES
The Boy in the Burning House © 2000 by Tim Wynne-Jones. Cover illustration by Greg Spalenka. Reprinted by permission of Groundwood Books/Douglas & McIntyre Ltd.; On *Tumbledown Hill* © 1998 by Tim Wynne-Jones. Illustrations © 1998 by Dusan Petricic. Reprinted by permission of Red Deer Press.

WERNER ZIMMERMANN
Brave Highland Heart © 1999 by Heather Kellerhals-Stewart. Illustrations © 1999 by Werner Zimmermann. Reprinted by permission of Stoddart Kids; *Snow Day* © 1999 by Werner Zimmermann. Reprinted by permission of Scholastic Canada Ltd.

ABOUT THE AUTHOR

Allison Gertridge is the author of the first edition of *Meet Canadian Authors and Illustrators*, as well as several other non-fiction books, including *Trim a Tree: 25 Christmas Ornaments You Can Make*. She has worked as a professional storyteller and as an editor, and now runs her own business, Think Publishing. She lives with her husband and two young children in Richmond Hill, Ontario.